SMALL COMPUTERS:
Exploring Their Technology and Future

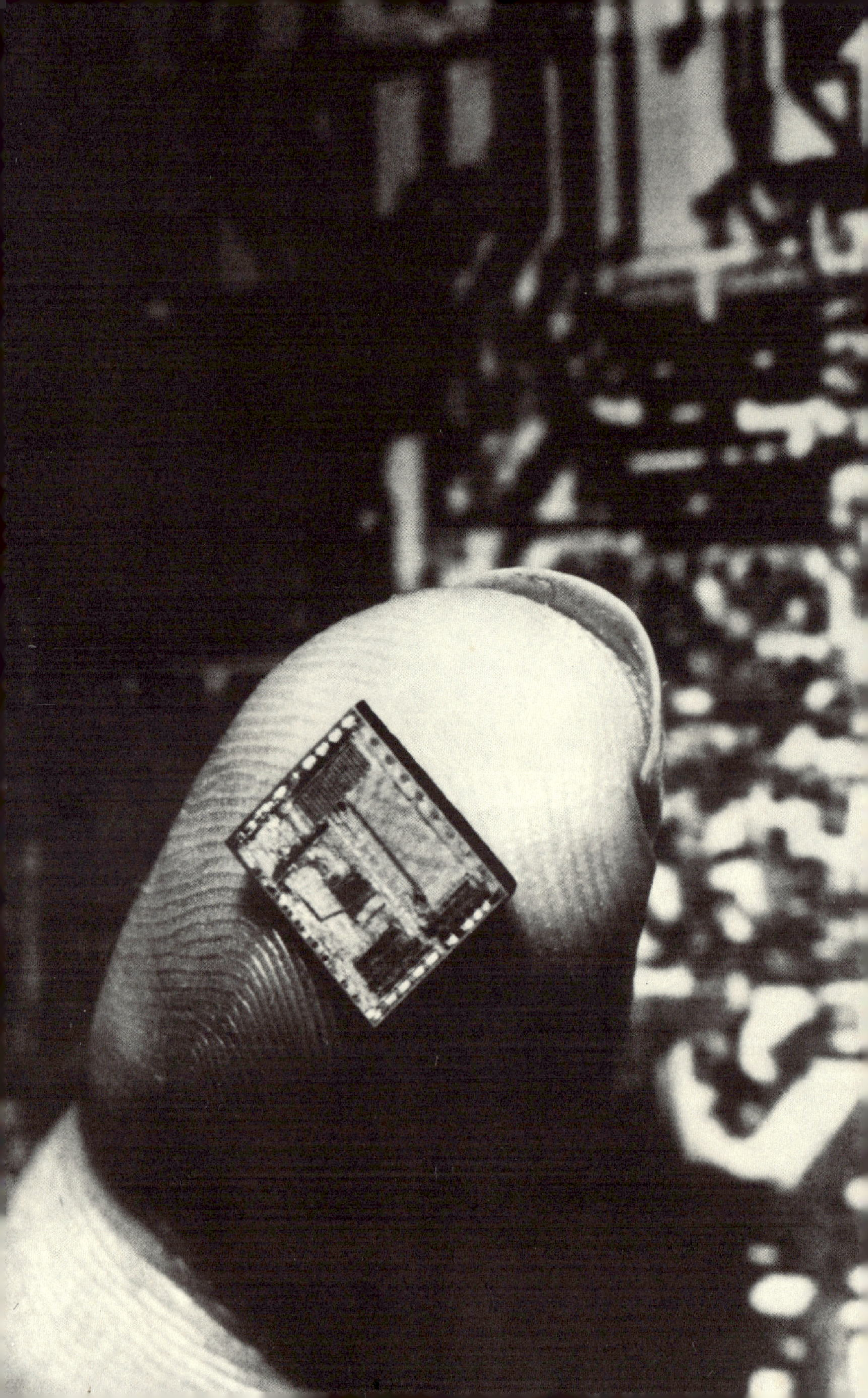

SMALL COMPUTERS: Exploring Their Technology and Future

by Fred D'Ignazio

A GROLIER COMPANY

Franklin Watts
New York/London/Toronto/Sydney/1981

Frontis: an 8-bit "computer-on-a-chip."

Jacket photograph courtesy of Atari. The computer model shown is an Atari 800.

Photographs courtesy of Intel Corporation: p. ii; Texas Instruments: p. 12; Votrax/HC Electronics, Inc.: p. 19; Mattel Electronics: p. 23 (top); Apple Computer Company: p. 23 (bottom); Atari Inc./ Taito America Corporation: p. 27; Commodore: p. 35; International Business Machines (IBM) Corporation: pp. 40 and 45; Digital Equipment Corporation: p. 42; Harvard University: p. 52 (data supplied by the National Planning Data Corporation); Atari Inc.: p. 56; Rosetta, Inc.: p. 67 (top and bottom); Battele Northwest Laboratories: p. 71; James A. Gupton Jr.: p. 77; Terrapin, Inc.: p. 82; New York Institute of Technology Computer Graphics Laboratory: p. 119 (top); Richard Shoup: p. 119 (bottom); Lear Siegler, Inc./Digital Engineering Inc.: p. 120.

Photograph on page 73 previously appeared in Tod Loofbourrow's book *How to Build a Computer-Controlled Robot* (Hayden Book Company, Inc.). It is reprinted here by permission of the publisher and The Art Works Photography.

Photograph on pages 83 and 84 are courtesy of Ellen C. Hildredth, author of an unpublished paper entitled "The Creation of Design" (Children's Learning Laboratory/MIT). Photographs by Chip Hoover.

Library of Congress Cataloging in Publication Data
D'Ignazio, Fred.
Small computers

Bibliography: p.
Includes index.
SUMMARY: Discusses the increasing use of small computers to perform routine household chores, store personal information, and do other tasks.
1. Minicomputers—Juvenile literature. 2. Microcomputers—Juvenile literature. 3. Electronic data processing—Juvenile literature. [1. Minicomputers. 2. Microcomputers. 3. Computers. 4. Electronic data processing] I. Title.
QA76.5.D4964 001.64'04 80–25094
ISBN 0–531–04269–3

Printed in the United States of America
5 4 3 2 1

CONTENTS

for
Babe and Libby D'Ignazio
your help and your love
have meant the world to me

ACKNOWLEDGMENTS

I am indebted to all those who helped make this book possible. I am particularly grateful to the following:

To Maury Solomon for her enthusiasm and patience, for her careful and creative editing, but most of all for not sending her "hit man" after me.

To Gregory Yob, Alan Kay, Adele Goldberg, Joseph Weizenbaum, Christopher Evans, and Seymour Papert for their vision of computers as miniature, controllable universes and as tools for learning and the imagination.

To Allen L. Wold for his ideas and suggestions for "The Enchanted Computer," the chapter on computer-assisted role-playing games.

To Chip Hoover, Alice Collette, and Dale Ingold for working so hard to prepare pictorial material for the book.

To Janet Letts D'Ignazio for her support and for helping me assemble the glossary, the appendices, and the entire manuscript.

To Marg Baldwin for putting me on the path to making this book a reality.

A GOOD MYSTERY BOOK

It is a hot, lazy afternoon in the middle of the summer. You are curled up on the couch in a cool corner of the house reading a mystery. You are totally absorbed in the book and have been trying to figure out who committed the gruesome murder that occurred in the first chapter.

You are nearing the climax. Soon you'll find out who did it. All of a sudden the writing on the page flickers, then disappears. In its place appears a man's face. "Hello," says the man. "You know me. I'm Tony Simone, the district attorney in your book. Do you remember me?"

"Yes," you answer.

"Have you read this book up to page one hundred and thirty-five?"

"Yes," you say again.

"Good. Then you've gotten to the point where I crack this case open. But before you read any further, I'd like you to answer a few questions. To start, who do you think killed Nash Goodknight after he left his girl friend's apartment?"

You have a hunch. "Was it Paul Callahan, Goodknight's ex-partner?"

"No!" shouts the D.A. "Callahan has an airtight alibi. Look at the evidence."

The man's face disappears from the book's page, and in its place appear several documents and photographs that convince you Callahan really does have an airtight alibi. Your hunch was wrong.

The D.A.'s face returns to the page. "Got a new suspect?" he asks.

"Ye–s–s," you say a bit more hesitantly this time. "How about. . . ."

This process goes on for several more minutes. Finally, after a number of guesses, the D.A. says, "Okay. That's enough. Now I want you to sit back and watch a pro in action. Maybe one of your suspects is the guilty party, maybe not. Finish the book, and you'll find out. And next time you read about one of my cases, pay more attention."

"Right," you say.

The man's face disappears for the last time. The words return to the page of the book. Eagerly you read the last chapter to see how the D.A. solves the crime and to find out who the real murderer is.

The little scenario above may seem strange to you. After all, books don't flash pictures, talk to you, or ask you questions. That is, books made out of *paper* don't. But books, along with thousands of other commonplace objects in our lives, are soon going to be transformed into something quite different from what we're used to today. In ten years or less, many books will no longer be published on paper. Instead they will be "stored" on a tiny chip of microelectronic circuitry, probably smaller than the fingernail on your pinkie. The book chip will be packaged inside a plastic cartridge that you can insert into your book player—complete with a screen, a small mike, an equally small speaker, and several buttons to allow you to "turn the pages" of the book and search for different types of information.

Once you buy your electronic book, you will turn on the book player and decide to either have the book read itself aloud or display the printed words on the screen for you to read yourself.

Reading a book is already an active experience. But in the future it will become even more so. Most books will "talk" to you, ask you questions about the story, and play music and show color pictures to accompany key parts. Some books will even stop periodically to ask you a question such as "Where do we go from here?," then continue with a plot designed to fit your answer.

Appliance Computers

Most small computers of the future will be appliance computers—tiny electronic chips hidden inside familiar objects such as stereos, telephones, typewriters, and books. The computer's *program*—its operating instructions—will be created, then frozen, at the factory. By the time the computer arrives at your home or classroom, its functions will already be permanently etched into its microscopic brain. When you use the appliance, you will be able to start and stop the computer's program, but you won't be able to change it. This will make the appliance computer a snap to operate but capable of performing only a limited number of tasks.

Will all small computers in the future be concealed inside appliances? Fortunately not. There is another type of small computer, one that could have a huge impact on how you learn and have fun.

You Give the Orders

How will the two kinds of computers differ? Most important of all, using the second kind, you will be able to write your own programs for the computer to obey. These programs might be as simple as solutions to arithmetic problems or as elaborate and creative as outer-space games, electronic paintings, models of a solar furnace, or original poems or musical compositions. Unlike the workhorse computers of the past, which were limited to storing and spitting out numbers, these small computers will have the ability to talk, listen, synthesize music, and produce colorful, animated pictures. In this book you will learn about the small computers of the present and of the future, and you will discover some of the fun and exciting ways in which they might be used.

A Book Preview

Section one of this book is about small computers of today. In chapter one you can read about the "explosion" of small computers. In chapters two and three you will learn how a digital watch computer is designed and programmed. Chapters four through seven take you on a whirlwind tour of small computers of all types, with a special focus on programmable computers. The first programmable small computers have already arrived.

Section two ("The Supercomputers") considers *hardware* (the mechanical side of computers). It begins with a look at the predicted rapid growth in ultraminiaturization of computer circuits and continues with a survey of the powerful small computers that are barely off the drawing boards, including the *array computer,* the *pipeline computer*, and the *Josephson computer,* an ultrafast computer with a supercooled brain.

Section three ("Computer Languages of the Future") deals with *software* (the programming commands that make computers work). It traces the evolution of computer languages and discusses the advantages (and disadvantages) of trying to get computers to speak English. It introduces you to one of the newest computer languages—SMALLTALK—and explains how a future version of this language and others like it will revolutionize the way you'll deal with computers in the future.

In section four ("Robots and Smart Computers") you will meet a variety of computerized robots and explore the limits of computer—and robot—intelligence. In the future, who's going to have the higher IQ, you or some superfast computer?

Section five ("Small Computers, the Future, and You") is fun and thought-provoking. In this section you will take a look into the future—at mind readers, electronic mail, intelligent houses, and invisible computers. You will learn how, by using the small computer's ability to *simulate* (build models), you will be able to create animated computer movies and play epic fantasy games that feature fierce dragons, fabulous treasures, and nonstop adventure.

Is the future for small computers all bright and rosy? No. There are some real problems and worries. In section six ("The Darker Side of What the Future Might Bring"), you'll meet computers used as weapons, the Information Burglar, and Big Brother. You'll also learn about the small computer's pitfalls, its drawbacks and limitations.

But the future's not all bleak, either. The text ends with a chapter on the ways in which you might use a small computer to compose music, perform thought-experiments, learn difficult subjects, and invent your own videogames. Remember, a small computer is more than a machine. It is a vehicle that can take you on a voyage of exploration—into the fantasy worlds inside your head or into the real world all around you.

TODAY'S COMPUTERS

Before we can explore the future of small computers, we need to examine the rapidly evolving present. What are the characteristics of today's small computers? How do they work? What are they good for? How do they differ from one another?

Just like Alice in Lewis Carroll's *Alice's Adventures in Wonderland,* the computer, by growing small, will be able to enter new worlds. But what disguise will it wear? Will it become an intelligent dishwasher? An electronic typewriter? A talking wristwatch?

Everyone has seen a digital watch or calculator—really a computer in disguise. But relatively few people know what the computer looks like on the inside, underneath all the buttons, the plastic, and the gleaming digital display. Few people know in addition that today's computers are built on a snowflake of *silicon,* the substance on beaches that sparkles on the sand when sunlight falls on it.

Many people feel that all small computers will ultimately wear disguises. But there is a debate among experts over the amount of computer control that should be left in the hands of the people who use them. Some experts want easy-to-use computer appliances, with narrow-minded special-purpose programs hidden and sealed inside the computer's brain. Others, including this author, feel that such a computer is too limited.

Powerful new computers that anyone can program are just becoming available. Let's look now at some of these machines and the important role they can play in education and entertainment.

THE SMALL-COMPUTER EXPLOSION

Have you ever seen a computer? Sure you have—in the form of an electronic game, a digital watch, or maybe a calculator. Today almost everyone has an opportunity to work with a computer. This was not the case just a few years ago. At that time computers were enormous machines, sometimes filling a room the size of your classroom at school. The computers had tall panels of blinking, multicolored lights, jumbles of crisscrossing, spaghetti-like wires, clacking printers violently disgorging mountainous stacks of paper, and formidable glass-and-steel cabinets housing tape drives that fizzed and whirled.

Perhaps you've visited a large-computer installation or seen a big computer in an old movie. These machines still exist today. They track and navigate satellites, handle phone calls, process the records of large corporations, predict the outcome of elections, and help scientists conduct experiments.

But after 1968 the large computers were no longer alone. At that time the *microcomputer* was born—a computer so small it can fit on a thin sliver of silicon about the size of a ladybug.

The invention of the microcomputer came about as a result of two decades of effort on the part of hundreds of scientists and engineers. Military, scientific, and spaceship computers were needed that were smaller and faster. To keep up with the needs, each year scientists invented new techniques for miniaturizing computer wires and squeezing them into tinier and tinier packages. Then, in 1968, M. E. Hoff, an engineer with Intel Corporation at Santa Clara, California, figured out a way to fit an entire computer onto a small square, or *chip,* of silicon. Hoff had invented the microcomputer, the world's first "computer on a chip."

The effect of the microcomputer was revolutionary and immediate. Big computers could now go faster, remember more, and process more, yet fit into the same amount of space. Small computers could be built and hidden inside factory equipment and business machines to make them "smarter" and more versatile.

By the mid-1970s, the microcomputer had sparked an

explosion of computerized consumer goods—hand-held calculators, digital watches, and electronic games were the most popular items. However, unlike most explosions, which are short-lived, this explosion has continued right up to the present and, if anything, is still gathering force. Today there are microcomputers in televisions, radios, and telephones; in typewriters, ovens, and washing machines; in stoplights, airplane navigation systems, and bathroom scales. The list could go on.

And no one knows where the explosion will end. We'll soon see electronic books; talking, computerized credit cards; and household robots. Even more incredible, a Dutch garment manufacturer recently announced that his company will soon begin production of computerized clothes!

DESIGNING A DIGITAL WATCH

Imagine that you are an electronics engineer working for a large company that manufactures digital watches. You've just been given the job of designing a small computer to go inside a digital watch. But before you begin, it's important to decide what functions the watch should have—what it should be able to do. To keep the watch simple, let's say it needs to have only one function—to tell time.

That's simple, right? Well, not exactly. Looking a little closer, you see that "telling the time" really means: (1) the watch must *learn* the exact time right now (within, say, a second); (2) the watch must *remember* the exact time; (3) as time passes—second by second—the watch must *change* the old time stored in its brain to the new time; and (4) the watch must *show* the new exact time (to the person wearing the watch).

Now let's take each of the four functions of the digital watch and decide what components the watch's computer will need in order to perform each function.

Function 1: Learning the Exact Time. How does the watch's computer know what the current exact time is? Someone has to tell it. If you're the one who owns the watch, you're the one who has to tell it. To do this, you need some means of communicating with the computer. You communicate with your digital watch computer by pressing two little buttons on its side. These buttons draw on the watch's battery and generate tiny charges of electricity that represent the exact time. The buttons allow you to *input* the exact time into the computer. So the first component the computer needs is *input.*

Function 2: Remembering the Exact Time. Let's say you have just entered the exact time (within a second) into the watch's computer. But if the computer doesn't remember the time (your input), it does no good at all. After all, what use is a watch that you have to enter the correct time in every second?

What does the computer need to remember the time? It needs a *memory,* and this memory must include a knowledge of when to enter the new time and when to erase the old time. In a small computer, this type of memory is called *RAM,* for *R*andom *A*ccess *M*emory. Inside a relatively large computer (like one in an air conditioner), RAM is stored on several tiny rectangular chips plugged into a circuit board. But inside a watch, where space is at a premium, RAM is stored—along with the entire computer!—on a chip that is less than a quarter of an inch on its side.

Dozens of tiny wires are soldered to the silicon chip by means of an extremely precise photochemical process. The wires crisscross much like the threads of a finely made fabric. At each intersection is a *capacitor,* a minute device capable of storing a single charge of electricity. In the computer's *binary,* or *machine, language,* the presence of a charge in a single capacitor represents a one. The absence of a charge represents a zero. A binary one or binary zero is called a *bit* (for *b*inary dig*it*). Several capacitors strung together can store the exact time coded in the binary language.

Thus your watch, in order to remember the time, must have memory.

Function 3: Keeping the Exact Time Current. Your watch remembers the current exact time because it is stored in RAM, the watch computer's memory. But how does the computer know when time passes, and how does it know *how* to replace the old time with the new?

This brings us to the heart of your watch's computer—to the heart of all small computers—the computer's brain. The brain inside a small computer is also a chip (or, in the case of a watch, part of a chip) and is known as the computer's *CPU* (*C*entral *P*rocessing *U*nit) or its *MPU* (*M*icro *P*rocessing *U*nit). Like the rest of the computer, CPU (or MPU) operates by processing charges of electricity that are fired through it in pulses, or bursts, of unbelievable speed.

What can the brain do? It can retrieve information from the computer's memory at a rate of eight bits (a *byte!*) at a time. It can reshape that information using simple arithmetic or logic. And it can store the new information in its memory.

CPU can also act on old information from memory and perform operations on new information. Or it can generate an electrical signal that can do anything from drive a piece of machinery to click the shutter on a camera or light up a giant baseball-stadium display board with the words, HOME RUN!! HOME RUN!!

Inside the brain itself there are several subunits, including one that performs arithmetic and handles the logic, a tiny "scratchpad" memory unit, and a crystal clock that oscillates, or vibrates, at least a million times a second!

So how does your watch keep the time? Simple. It keeps tab on its own clock, and after every million clock vibrations, the computer adds a new second to the old time stored in its RAM memory.

Thus, in order to keep the exact time current, the computer needs a brain.

Function 4: Showing the New Exact Time. You have a problem. Your watch is doing a great job keeping the time. That time is stored as a sequence of electrical charges inside the computer's memory. But stored in that form, it's not doing you one bit of good, is it?

So how do you get the time? First you need the time *translated* into regular old decimal numbers that you can understand. Second, you need to have those numbers *displayed* where you can see them.

If you owned a *voltmeter,* it would be easy to translate

the on-off charges of electricity into ones and zeros. But then you'd have to decode a long string of ones and zeros into decimal numbers (numbers from "0" to "9") that represented the current time in hours, minutes, and seconds.

If you had the key to the computer's binary code, you could do this yourself also. But when you finally finished converting all the numbers and figuring out the time, it would probably be half an hour too late!

But unlike you, the computer is fast. Why not let it translate the time? And in fact it can, in an infinitesimal fraction of a second. Then, as soon as the time is translated into something you can understand, the computer displays it on a picture screen.

With larger computers, the picture screen might be a flat, *plasma-ray device,* with messages from the computer that glow in bright orange. Or the screen might be a *CRT,* or *C*athode *R*ay *T*ube, much like the picture tube on your TV.

In the case of the watch, the screen is only a thin window on the watch's face, probably an *LCD* (*L*iquid *C*rystal *D*isplay) or *LED* (*L*ight-*E*mitting-*D*iodes). In any case, the screen completes the last major function of your watch computer, display.

A Look at the Whole Watch

In this chapter we designed the major parts of a small computer, a computer that drives a digital watch. When the parts are put together, the computer operates properly and enables the watch to perform its function.

The *input devices* (the buttons) enable you to enter the initial exact time into the computer. The computer stores the exact time in its *memory* (RAM). The computer *brain* (CPU) keeps the time up to date. And the current exact time is displayed on the computer's *output device* (the LED or LCD screen).

PROGRAMMING A DIGITAL WATCH

In the last chapter you played the role of an electronics engineer and designed a small computer for a digital watch. Now the watch has been built. But is it ready to be shipped

MOS MICROCOMPUTER

1 READ ONLY MEMORY

2 RANDOM ACCESS MEMORY

3 CONTROL DECODE

4 ARITHMETIC LOGIC UNIT

5 CLOCK

6 INPUT/OUTPUT DECODE

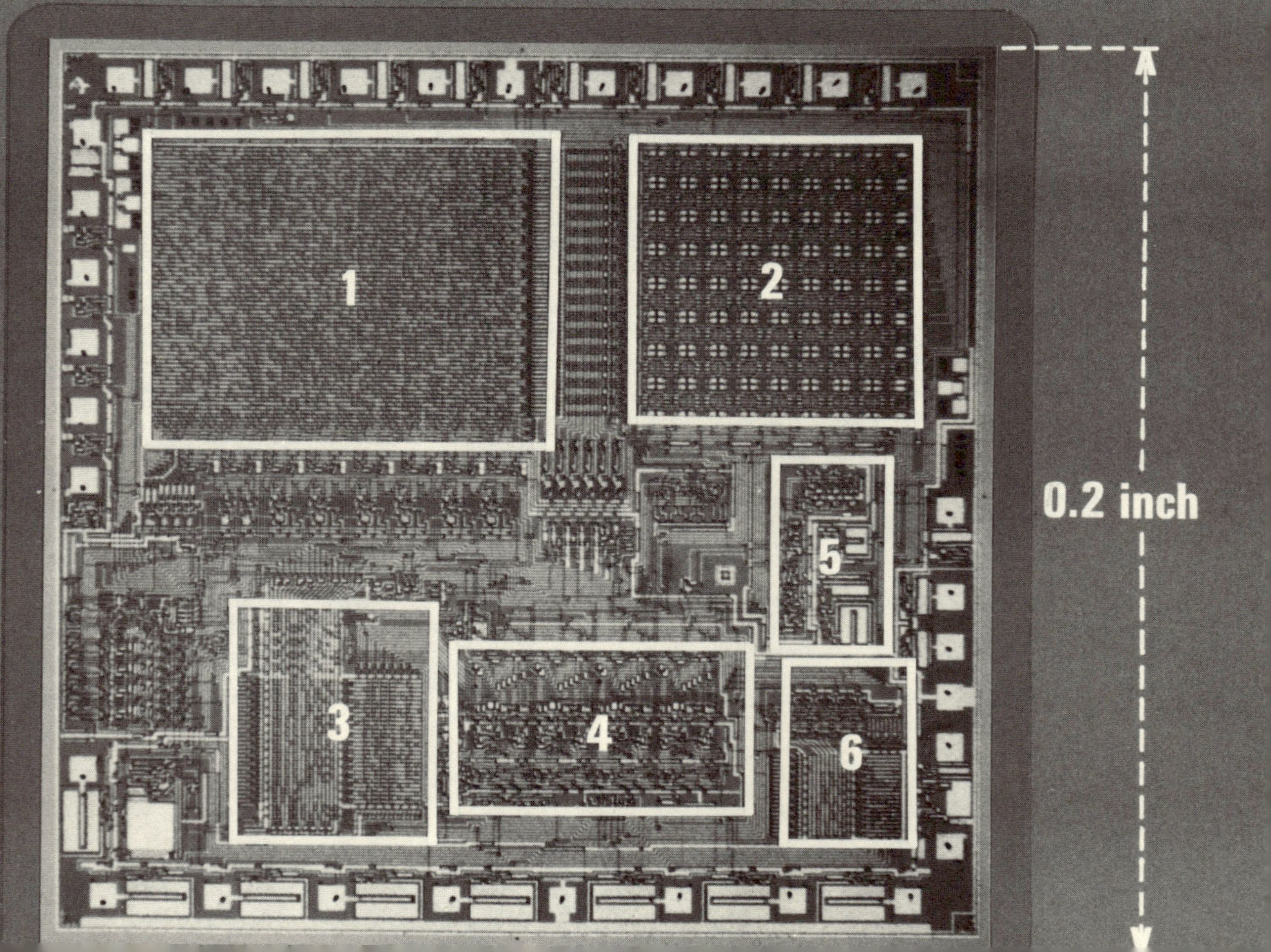

to the stores? No. First the computer needs a program—a set of instructions stored permanently in its memory. The program drives the computer, and the computer makes the watch tell time.

In this chapter imagine that you are a computer programmer at the watch-manufacturing plant. Your boss has just given you the job of designing the program that will make the watch's computer tell time.

Remember, there are two sides to every computer—hardware and software. Last chapter we looked at hardware, the "nuts and volts" of small computers—the brain, the memory, the input and output devices. This chapter is about software, the instructions that bring the computer to life and make it perform a task such as telling the time.

Remember the four functions involved in telling time? First, input of the initial exact time. Second, storage of that time in memory. Third, calculation of a new exact time (the current time). And, fourth, output of the exact time to a display.

To make the computer perform all of the above functions, you need to give it instructions. Taken together, the instructions should make the computer tell time. When the instructions are written in a language the computer can recognize, and when all the instructions together get the computer to perform a common task, they make up what is known as a *program.* The program is stored in the computer's memory. And all the computer's programs, taken together, are known as its *software.*

ROM: The Computer's Permanent Memory

The digital watch contains a special-purpose computer. It needs only one program, a program to make the computer tell time. That program is stored in memory known as *ROM* (*R*ead *O*nly *M*emory).

A computer like the one shown here, with its component parts, is often used in digital watches.

ROM, though built somewhat differently from RAM, is like RAM in that its programs and information can be retrieved extremely rapidly. However, the information stored in ROM is stored there *permanently* and cannot be erased without the use of special equipment. Each time the computer is shut off, its information and programs disappear from RAM. In ROM they remain intact.

After you write the watch's program for ROM, you use a special device with an ultraviolet light. This device "burns" your program into ROM. And once in ROM, the program becomes a permanent part of the watch's computer—up and running the moment the computer is "plugged" into its power source, a tiny, circular battery.

Choosing the Right Language

All information and instructions inside the computer are stored and processed as on-off or high-low charges of electricity. These binary electrical signals represent the internal, or machine, language built into the computer's CPU (Central Processing Unit), or brain. An "on" or "high" charge represents a binary "1," and an "off" or "low" charge represents a "0." Taken together, a sequence of charges—a string of one and zero bits—represent specially coded information and commands. Who does this coding, this conversion of decimal numbers and English words and letters into ones and zeros, and, ultimately, into electrical charges? The computer itself, with the help of special translator programs known as *monitors, compilers,* and *interpreters.* These programs feature a wide range of Englishlike, arithmetic, and word- or letter-handling commands commonly referred to as *computer languages.* With many of these languages, such as *LOGO, SMALLTALK, PASCAL, BASIC,* and *ASSEMBLER,* you can do almost as many things as you could do using the computer's own cumbersome and awkward machine language. Yet the commands are easy to use and understand, and they are amazingly powerful.

Writing the Watch Program

When you were given the job to program the watch's computer, you were told to use *APPLIANCE,* a language that resembles English.* And, remember, though a watch's software might consist of several programs (including programs to tell the current date, programs to set and ring an alarm, "chronograph" programs, and so on) your assignment consisted of writing only one program—a program to make the watch tell time.

What commands should be in your program? First, you need an INPUT (current time) command to get the initial exact time into the computer. Here "INPUT" is the actual command to the computer, and "current time" is the *data* to be entered into the computer. This data is the actual time you enter (by pressing the buttons) when you are setting your watch.

Next, you might use a STORE command to stash the time away in the computer's memory.

Third, you've got to make the computer come up with a new exact time. That'll take some doing. Right now, let's say you use an "umbrella" command such as COMPUTE TIME. This command directs the computer to a "subprogram" nested at the end of the main program.

Next, you want the computer to translate the time from binary to decimal numbers. This requires a number of separate steps—too many to go into in this chapter. We'll use another umbrella command, such as TRANSLATE TIME.

Finally, you want the computer to display the exact time for you to read. Here try a command such as OUTPUT TIME.

Subroutines to Handle Details

Whenever you write a program, you first take care of the main functions or tasks, then worry about the details later. This approach keeps your thinking organized and your priorities clear.

One way to avoid getting bogged down is to use *subroutines.* Subroutines are like little programs nested inside of big programs. Subroutines are for doing the dirty work—all the nitty-gritty, complicated things you want to keep out of your main program.

---

* APPLIANCE is not a real computer language.

You can use subroutine commands as special umbrella commands in the body of your main program. When the CPU retrieves a subroutine command from memory, it knows to look elsewhere in the program for a list of the detail commands.

In your program, when the CPU sees COMPUTE TIME, it doesn't recognize it as a regular command, so it searches the end of the program looking for a subroutine.

Reviewing the Whole Program

After you finish writing your program, you need to name it. How about something simple, like WATCH?

Here is what your entire program looks like with all the commands and subroutines:

```
PROGRAM: WATCH

change  INPUT (current time)
        STORE TIME
new     COMPUTE TIME
        TRANSLATE TIME
        OUTPUT TIME
        GO BACK TO "new"

SUBROUTINE: COMPUTE TIME

clock   ADD 1 TO CLOCK VIBRATION COUNT
        DOES CLOCK VIBRATION COUNT = 1,000,000?
        IF NOT GO BACK TO "clock"

        FETCH CURRENT TIME FROM MEMORY
        ADD 1 TO CURRENT TIME
        STORE CURRENT TIME BACK IN MEMORY
        SET CLOCK VIBRATION COUNT TO 10

        END OF SUBROUTINE

SUBROUTINE: TRANSLATE TIME

        (commands)

        END OF SUBROUTINE

END OF WATCH PROGRAM
```

Using the ultraviolet-light device, you "burn" your program into ROM to store it permanently inside the computer and then test it so you can be sure you've done everything right.

THE MANY KINDS OF SMALL COMPUTERS

There is an explosion of small computers throughout our society and, indeed, throughout the world. Small computers are being employed in almost every form of human endeavor from the control of nuclear reactors to on-the-spot analyses of archaeological artifacts found in remote regions of the world. And this is just the beginning. Small computers have only been around a few years. The uses that lie ahead for them are limited only by people's imagination and ingenuity.

But even now there are ways to distinguish among various types of small computers. When you hear of a particular small computer, there are some questions you might want to ask. For example:

Is it a Special-Purpose or General-Purpose Computer? A computer is, by its nature, a general-purpose machine. That is, given unlimited memory, processing power, and time, a computer can solve any problem, perform any activity, or obey any set of commands that can be clearly described. This extraordinary versatility is why computers are at work solving problems and storing and reshaping information in all areas of daily life. Computers help produce the magazines and the books—or the comic books—that you read. They help train your favorite athletes. They filter, alter, and refine the songs played by your favorite musicians.

On the other hand, the computer becomes a special-purpose machine when its designers feed it only one program, as in the case of the digital watch. Then a single program endlessly cycles through the computer's brain, and the computer's functions are strictly limited by the commands that make up the program.

The digital watch is, of course, a special-purpose computer and is a good example of the new breed of solid-state appliances that include computerized ovens, bathroom scales, air conditioners, and so on.

What are some other types of special-purpose computers? Hand-held electronic games are an example of special-purpose computers—games such as Mattel's *Brainbaffler* and Coleco's *Head-to-Head Football.*

Special-purpose computers also include electronic language translators such as Craig's M100, electronic toys such as Playskool's Alphie the Robot, and electronic learning aids such as Texas Instruments' Speak & Spell.

Finally, a rapidly growing number of special-purpose computers are being made for handicapped, infirm, and elderly people. There is the C-Phone electronic typewriter, which allows deaf people to make and receive telephone calls, the Kurzweil Reading Machine, which reads books aloud for blind people, and the Optacom, which allows severely handicapped people to create typed messages simply by looking at different letters on a picture screen.

Is the Computer Programmable or Nonprogrammable? The problem here is that most nonprogrammable computers appear to be programmable. A videogame computer gives you a whole range of game "commands" you can choose from. A microwave oven computer lets you "program" the cooking of a roast. A marvelous robot toy called Big Trak (from Milton Bradley) gives you a number of "commands" to let you "program" the robot truck's movement across your living room floor.

And it's true. You are in the driver's seat. You can make Big Trak go in any sequence of directions you choose (up to nineteen "program steps"). You can program your oven to burn the roast—if you want to. And, if you're skillful or just plain lucky, you can issue game commands to whip the pants off your videogame computer.

But in spite of all this seeming control, you are not programming. You are simply choosing among the limited

The Phonic Mirror HandiVoice computer put out by HC Electronics, Inc., one of the small-computer devices recently developed to aid handicapped people.

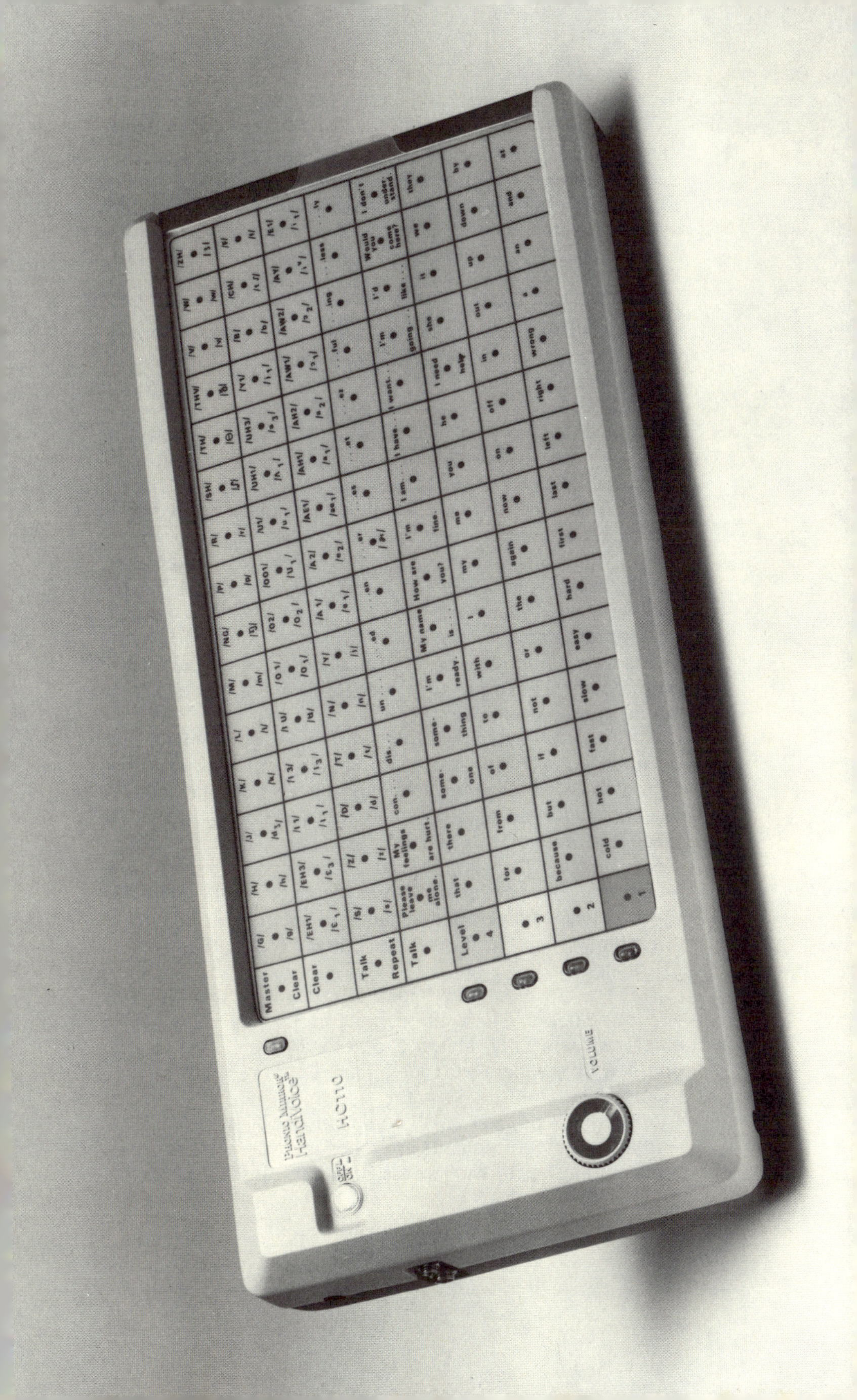

Phonic Mirror
HandiVoice
HC110
VOLUME

set of options provided by a single program housed inside a special-purpose computer. For example, what if you wanted Big Trak to play a game of *Space Invaders* with you? Or the oven computer to store the names of the presidents for a history exam? What would happen if you tried to program your videogame computer to help you solve some problems in your math homework?

Absolutely nothing. You couldn't do it. Special-purpose computers are terrific for doing one thing, but they are not programmable.

Can the Computer Handle Words As Well As Numbers? Letters and words are symbols. Numbers are symbols. The computer is a whiz at symbols.

Letters and words are manipulated according to certain rules of grammar, record keeping, or whatever. Numbers are manipulated according to the rules of mathematics. Those rules—*all* rules—can be programmed into the computer.

A programmable general-purpose computer can handle words as well as numbers. But many special-purpose computers can't. That's because their program will accept only words or only numbers.

Here's an example of a word-oriented computer. A business suite in the Watergate housing complex in Washington, D.C., is occupied by a group that claims to have the first paperless office. All records and documents in the office are created, stored, processed, copied, and mailed electronically. This is referred to as *computerized word processing.* All of the word-processing computers in this office can accept and store numbers as part of the text of a document or record. But few can perform arithmetic on the numbers.

There are also many types of computers that will only accept numbers. Biorhythm computers usually allow you to enter numbers only. Milton Bradley's Comp IV has a keyboard with numbers but no letters. Coleco's Zodiac computer is the same.

The most popular small computer of all—the calculator—is a magnificent number cruncher (processor), but it will have nothing to do with words or letters. Inside the calculator is a tiny computer, and inside the computer is a single set of instructions. These instructions give the computer the following abilities: (1) the ability to accept numbers punched in on the small keyboard; (2) the ability to perform arithmetic on those numbers; and (3) the ability to print out the answer.

But the newer calculators can do a lot more than this. Take the HP-41C calculator put out by Hewlett-Packard. You can make this little computer do some pretty high-powered arithmetic. And it can also be programmed. You enter your programs into the HP-41C from *magnetic cards* or by waving an *optical wand* over a printed page. You can program it to play musical tones, solve numerical problems, and even play games.

Does this make the HP-41C a general-purpose computer? In fact, it does—a general-purpose numerical computer.

Which Computers Have Bells and Whistles? The answer to this question is easy. Soon *all* computers will have bells and whistles. They are just too attractive to pass up.

What are some of the bells and whistles, and which computers have them now? Bells and whistles are actually fancy extras, or *add-ons,* that come with or can be attached to the basic computer. They include colorful *graphics* (pictures), musical tones, synthetic voices, elaborate game panels and game controls, and microphones that allow you to give verbal commands to the computer.

Many small computers already have these add-ons, for example the musical calculator mentioned above. In addition, there now are talking digital watches for blind people and talking, intelligent chess, backgammon, and bridge computers such as Boris, Chess Challenger, and Gammonmaster. There are talking language computers, such as Texas Instruments' Speak & Spell, and TI's talking translator. And there are dozens of talking, buzzing, beeping, or musical electronic toys.

Finally, there's another add-on that's very important—the ROM *cartridge,* or ROM *pack.* Inside the Read Only Memory pack is a canned game, learning, or entertainment program ready to be plugged into the computer and run.

Tired of the old program and ready for a new challenge? Pop out the old ROM pack and pop in a new one.

All sorts of small computers now come with slots for tape cartridges and ROM packs. These computers include Atari's Video Computer, TI's Speak & Spell, several calculators and toys, and Mattel's Intellivision. Also included in this group are some of the early small programmable computers, notably the APF Imagination Machine and the Exidy Sorceror.

THE GREAT COMPUTER DEBATE

What if you got a phone call tomorrow and someone told you that you had just won a new stereo in a national sweepstakes? You'd be pretty happy, right?

Then what if you were told that you had to choose between two types of stereos. The first one had lots of buttons, levers, and dials. It was a bit complicated to operate, but you could adjust it to suit your musical tastes and get it to produce fabulous sound.

The second stereo was a lot simpler to operate—there was just one button and a couple of dials. Although the sound was still good, it was not fantastic. And there was no way to "customize" your music to your tastes and to the type of record or tape you were playing.

The question is, which stereo would you choose?

What do stereos have to do with computers? It is true that many stereos already come with lasers, radio controls, and tiny computers inside that let you "program" your music to play in any order you choose. The two types of stereos in the example above, however, are similar to the two types of computers involved in a debate raging in the

Above: Mattel's Intellivision computer, with canned game programs that can be hooked into any ordinary television set.

Below: an Apple II computer with its many possible "add-ons."

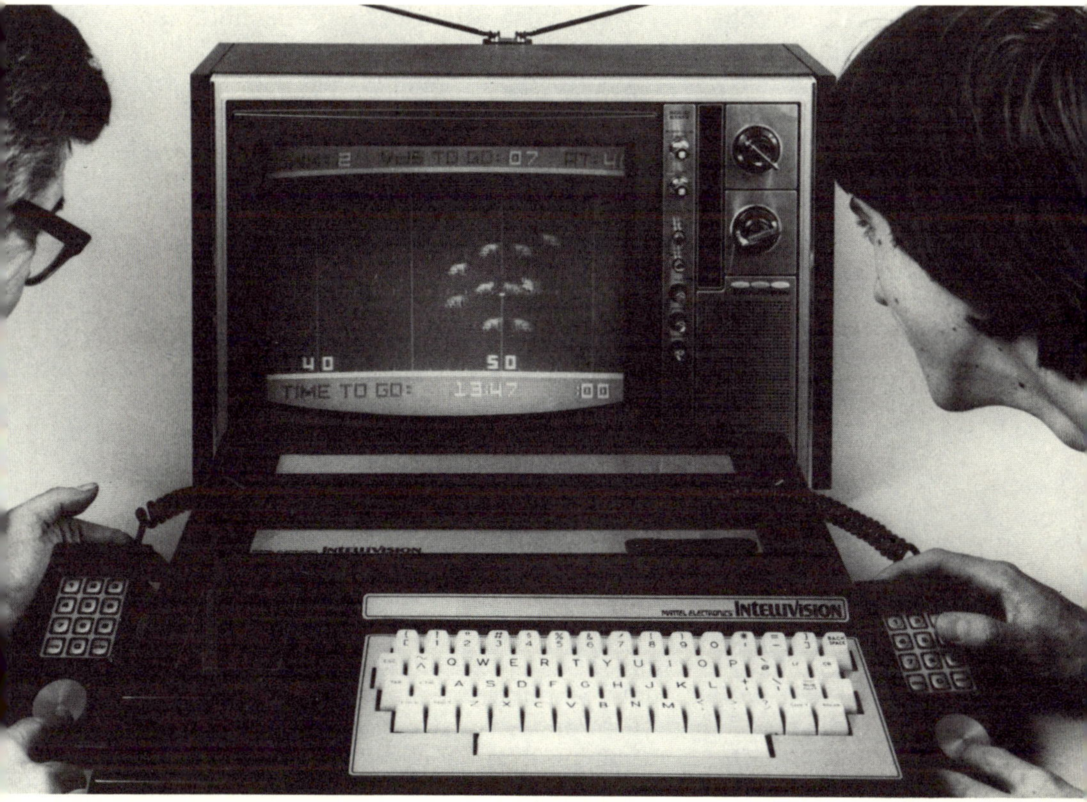
TIME TO GO: 13:47 :00
40
50
INTELLIVISION
MATTEL ELECTRONICS INTELLIVISION

Apple II Reference Manual
January 1978
APPLESOFT
apple software bank
APPLE II
apple II
disk II

field of consumer electronics—the nonprogrammable computers versus the programmable computers.

On one side there are companies and experts who claim that eventually all small computers will disappear inside other appliances, just as electric motors have "disappeared" inside dozens of business and household appliances. People won't ever say, "The computer did this," or "The computer did that." Instead, they'll say, "The typewriter did this," or "The stove did that."

According to the experts, this is for the best, since basically people are afraid of computers. They think computers are whimsical, possibly evil, and definitely too complicated. People have no desire in the world to learn how computers operate or to program computers themselves.

Thus, the solution is to hide the computer inside something else. Feed the computer only one program, such as "Wash the clothes," or "Cook the roast." Lock the program inside the computer so the user can't change it. Then, perhaps most important, keep the controls simple—not too many buttons or dials!

There is another side to this debate, of course, described earlier. Other experts and some other companies claim that hiding all computers and outfitting them with limited, one-shot programs is like choosing the second stereo over the first. Sure, the product is less threatening and somewhat easier to use, but it is nowhere near as exciting, as versatile, or as responsive to the individual who owns or uses the product.

In the case of the computer, hiding it and forcing it to run someone else's program robs the user of the chance to mold the computer to individual needs and desires. It also sacrifices most of the computer's powerful potential for problem solving, teaching, and entertaining.

A programmable computer encourages people to program on their own. Thus it is a powerful stimulus to planning, logical thinking, creativity, and invention.

BUILDING MODELS WITHOUT GLUE

Why should you learn to program? One reason might be because programming is getting easier and easier. New computer languages such as LOGO and SMALLTALK (see section three) make it simpler—and more exciting—than ever to learn to program. But to really answer this question, you first need to answer another question—what *is* a computer?

The first computers—in the 1940s and 1950s—were the leviathan-sized tools of science and the military. It was these machines that fostered the image of computers as number crunchers, numerical geniuses, and mathematical marvels.

Later, in the 1960s and 1970s, newer and faster models were employed in business and industry, and a new view of computers arose. Now computers were seen as cold, blundering, despotic machines that turned people into numbers, sent consumers fictitious and arbitrary bills, and bumped factory workers off the assembly line to replace them with robots.

This brings us nearly to the present and yet another new image of computers. This new image is due to the tiny microcomputer and its appearance in hundreds of consumer electronic products—from toys and typewriters to home security systems and barroom games. Now, increasingly, computers are seen as a gimmick or gadget—a marvelous device invented for the benefit of consumers. There is a sense of anticipation spreading. "Where," everyone wonders, "will computers pop up next?"

Finally, there are other images of computers that come from the entertainment world. Films such as *2001: A Space Odyssey* and *Demon Seed* picture computers as a superior but fatally flawed and evil form of intelligence. The *Star Wars* series and Disney's *Black Hole* portray robots and computers as trusted servants of humankind or its most feared enemies, depending on who controls them.

Build Your Own Universe

Our current images of the computer will undoubtedly fade and be replaced by newer images as computer technology sprints forward and as computers filter more rapidly into our society and into our lives. But there is a new image of computers already on the horizon that is bound to become more widespread in the years ahead. This is an image of the computer as an electronic genie, a master model builder, or the ultimate dream machine.

Where does this image come from? It comes directly from the new breed of programmable small computers now appearing in the classroom and in the home. You can talk to these computers and make them talk back. You can use them to compose and play music. You can generate colorful, animated images on their TV-like picture screens. But most important of all, you can use all these features to program a computer to act as a gateway to the universe or as a window into the universe of your own mind.

The most wonderful attraction of these new general-purpose programmable computers is their ability to create a model of almost anything that exists or can be imagined. The model would not be built from plastic, wood, or glue but from the knowledge you possess, the ideas inside your head, and the program inside the computer. The model would appear on the computer screen and could be accompanied by sound effects, voices, or music from the computer's speakers.

Just what is a model? A model is a miniature representation of something real or imagined. A photograph or portrait of a person is a model of the real human being. A model airplane may be a plastic-and-glue imitation of a real airplane. Book trilogies such as J. R. R. Tolkien's *Lord of the Rings* are models of fantasy worlds created purely from the author's imagination.

Board games are models. So are electronic games such as Atari's *Parachute Jump,* Parker Brothers' *Stop Thief* ®, and Mattell's *Football.* How exciting each game is depends on how realistic the model is, because the more realistic it is, the more you feel you are really there.

For example, when you begin playing Taito Corporation's *Space Invaders* game, you are somewhere in deep space facing a massive alien attack. All of a sudden, hordes of multicolored creatures crowd onto the picture screen and begin to move toward you. Their advance is relentless. Then you see, from across the screen, flying saucers also heading toward you. Armed with lasers, you try to beat back the attack, but as soon as you've destroyed all the attackers, a new force appears even nearer to you than the last.

Space Invaders, here being
played on an Atari Video Computer,
is one of the most popular
new games of the small-computer age.

By the time the game is over, even if you have somehow destroyed all the attackers and won the game, you are liable to be sweaty, shaken, and exhausted. You were almost totally absorbed in the game (or model) due to its fast action and intense realism. In fact it is these two characteristics that have made *Space Invaders* the most popular computer videogame in the world.

But if games like *Space Invaders* can bring you models that are this exciting, why should you want to program models on your own? This is actually an easy question to answer. Just think for a second of what programming really is. According to computer specialist Greg Yob:

> If you can program your
> computer, here is a tiny universe
> in which you can be God. Within
> the realms of expression that the
> computer can provide, you can build
> a world, define its laws, and watch
> the universe unfold. As your whim
> dictates, you can intervene at any
> time, and if you desire, the
> history of the universe can be
> changed and rewritten at will.
> Such a power this is!

With a programmable computer you can invent a game, build a model, or create a universe, based on any book you've ever read, any movie you've ever seen, or any song or piece of music that ever inspired you. It's like being a scriptwriter, director, producer, and lead actor, all at the same time. It's up to you to create the story, the heroes, the villains, the action, the pictures, and the sound.

With older, plastic models, you were dependent on the model company to supply you with the basic kit. Not so with a small computer. Using a computer you can build models from scratch, and the possibilities are endless.

What else might you model? How about something simple, such as a rotating, multicolored cube? Or something awesome and complex, perhaps an exploding volcano, complete with deafening roars, black, billowing smoke, showers of sparks and cinders, and gushing lava?

As your knowledge grows, your models can become more realistic, more sophisticated, and more absorbing. Also, models can be a tremendous learning tool. They can stimulate powers of invention you never knew you had. One fellow, for example, invented an outer-space game and programmed it on his computer. After playing the game over and over, he grew tired of calculating the angle of trajectory that would allow his spaceship to warp into hyperspace. So he put his mind to work and, after considerable effort, reinvented the protractor. (This, by the way, was a pretty amazing feat. After all, it took a genius to invent the protractor the first time.)

So we're finally getting back to the question we asked at the beginning of the chapter: Why should you learn to program? The answer, of course, is to build models—models in the form of games or computer movies and cartoons, models to recreate nature, or models of fantasy universes inhabited by monsters and aliens and all the weird and zany characters only you could invent.

THE EARLY SMALL COMPUTERS

Intelligence is sometimes defined as a person's ability to cope with the unexpected—to handle new situations or manage new tasks. It's much the same with computers. For computers, intelligence is the ability to handle different tasks. Most hand-held game and appliance computers have only a limited amount of intelligence. They can do only what was programmed into them at the factory. Other computers, such as videogames, are more intelligent because they have a number of programs. These programs come on ROM cartridges and tape cassettes and can be plugged into the computer one at a time. Even here, though, the computer's intelligence is limited by the number of manufactured programs available.

Both of these types of computers come with some intelligence already programmed in. But there's no way to teach the computers and make them any smarter. The new general-purpose programmable computers are just the opposite. They often come with no intelligence at all, but you can *teach* them. How smart they become is limited only by the effort and imagination that goes into the programs you write.

These computers have tools to help you teach them. For example they have a monitor language that lets you create, change, and erase program and data files. They usually have a programming language, such as SMALLTALK, LOGO, BASIC, PASCAL, FORTH, or PILOT, which lets you create your own programs using special commands. And more and more, they come with graphics, voice, and music languages, which let you build models, draw pictures, compose and play music, and talk and listen to your computer. All of these tools help you make the computer smarter—and more exciting.

The remainder of this chapter is a survey of today's general-purpose programmable computers.

Something New: Mass Memory

When you designed the watch computer earlier, you learned about the computer's main memory—its RAM (Random Access Memory). You learned that the computer's brain (or CPU) uses RAM to store important information (data) that is needed by an active, currently running program.

Later, you programmed the watch computer. At that time you learned about a new kind of memory—ROM (Read Only Memory). ROM, you learned, was permanent memory. It was where your watch program would be stored.

Then you learned about a new kind of ROM—ROM packs and ROM cartridges. You learned that these were used to store canned games and other programs and that you could easily pop them in and out of a small computer.

A watch computer—a computer on a chip—needs only two kinds of memory—RAM and ROM. But a larger computer usually comes with a third kind of memory—*mass memory.* Mass memory comes in many forms—as tape cassettes, flexible disks, hard disks, magnetic-bubble chips, and so on.

Why is mass memory important? A small computer lets you store your own programs and data in RAM. But when you turn the computer off, everything that was stored in RAM is erased. If you have a huge game program you just spent an hour entering into RAM, the last thing you want is to see it disappear. That's where mass memory comes in. It is used to store the programs and information you had in RAM while the computer is turned off. Then, when you turn the computer back on, you can copy the programs from mass memory back into RAM. And, if you want, you can erase the copies in mass memory so you can reuse the space later.

What might you store in mass memory? First, you can use it to store different computer translator or language programs (such as BASIC or PASCAL). These represent part of the small computer's software. Second, you can use mass memory to store your files and records—all the information you keep on the computer. Third, you use mass memory to store all of your programs—your game programs, homework programs, models, and so on.

What does mass memory look like? The most popular—and the cheapest—kind of mass memory is the *tape cassette* or *tape recorder.* Another kind is the *flexible disk*—the floppy disk or diskette. The disk fits inside a disk drive, where it is rotated at high speed. Disk storage is more expensive than tape storage, but there are significant advantages to disk storage, including ease of use and speed.

In the future more and more small computers will come with hard (high-speed nonremovable) disks and with magnetic-bubble memory. We will talk more about each of these kinds of memory in section two.

The Computer Store

Computers you can program are sold in department, electronics, and discount stores. They are also sold in stores that specialize in small computers.

A small-computer store is a lot like a stereo store. It's a place where people interested in small computers gather to talk. It sells whole computer systems and books and magazines on how to build and program small computers. It also sells dozens of computer parts and accessories—microprocessor (CPU) chips, memory (RAM and ROM) chips, and logic (And, Or, and Not) gates. There are canned programs, computer kits, computer picture screens, keyboards, floppies, and tape cassettes.

The Cadillacs and Volkscomputers

Deluxe small computers, the Cadillacs of the line, can cost up to several thousand dollars. Who would pay that kind of money for a small computer? Mostly serious computer hobbyists, doctors, lawyers, and small businesses.

There are many computers that cost much less than the Cadillacs—we'll call them the Volkscomputers—yet are still complete computers. They have a keyboard, sometimes a picture screen (usually black and white), a CPU, RAM and ROM memories, and a tape recorder or a minifloppy disk drive.

These computers often come with a monitor program stored permanently in their ROM memory. The program begins running as soon as the computer is turned on and can help you enter new program commands into the computer as well as help you store programs and data on tape cassette and disk files.

Volkscomputers have add-ons too. These include extra memory and attachments that can enable you to draw color pictures or make sound effects or music. Canned game programs such as Tiger Tank, Breakout, President's Quiz, and Lunar Lander are also available (stored on tape cassette or floppy).

It usually pays to find out which parts are add-ons and which come with the basic computer. For some Volkscomputers, the picture screen, the tape recorder, and even the computer's metal case and power supply are "extras."

Small-Computer Kits

If even the Volkscomputers are too expensive for you, don't give up. Consider a kit. Some kits cost as little as a good tape recorder. They don't come with any attachments or fancy parts, yet they do assemble into complete computers. They have a CPU, a limited amount of RAM and ROM memories, and probably a little LED (light-emitting diode) display.

A kit usually comes with a good part of the computer already constructed. It remains for you to plug in and solder the *Dual Inline Packages (DIPs)*, which contain the chips, and other electronic components—resistors, diodes, etc.—onto a plastic *printed circuit board* (*PCB*).

Assembling a small computer can be an exciting class or family project. It will teach you a lot about the computer's parts. And it is not hard to do. It just requires some patience.

If you are planning to build a computer from a kit, remember to be on the lookout for extra parts. After you have assembled the basic computer, you might want to add a regular (letters and numbers) keyboard, a picture screen or TV monitor, and a tape recorder. These items don't usually come in the original kits.

Game and Learning Computers

Game and learning computers cost somewhere between Cadillacs and Volkscomputers. They are very much like videogame computers, except you can program them yourself if you choose to.

These computers have the same basics as the other general-purpose small computers—RAM, ROM, a CPU, and a keyboard. Sometimes they come with a color picture screen. More often, you buy the computer separately and, using a special attachment, plug it in to your own TV.

Game and learning computers generally allow you to draw color or black-and-white pictures. You can draw with up to 256 colors (though 12 or 16 colors is the standard) and with very fine detail—up to 250,000 dots, or *pixels,* per picture.

These computers come with large and still-growing libraries of canned programs, programs such as Colormath, The Great American Probability Machine, Hangman, Star Wars, Blackjack, Othello, and Chess. Also, there are lots of useful add-ons, such as floppy disk drives, a calendar/clock, a voice-recognition unit (so you can talk to the computer), a speech synthesis unit (so your computer can talk back), and accessories such as a Graphics Input Tablet that allows you to trace maps, pictures, and drawings and have them displayed on the computer's picture screen—with any changes or improvements you wish to make.

What to Watch for

New and more powerful small computers are constantly being introduced. But with all the products on the market and with all the razzle-dazzle advertising, it's hard to tell which features are important and which are not. Here, then, is a brief guide for selecting a small computer of the future.

First, in order to be really useful, the computer must be general-purpose, programmable, and capable of handling words and letters as well as numbers. It must be able to do anything you want it to do. Are the computer's languages limited and special-purpose, or can you use them to create games and build models? Be sure to find out which kinds of general-purpose languages come with the computer. Some of the most popular today are BASIC, PILOT, FORTH, PASCAL, APL, LISP, and C.

Second, look for computers with quality graphics. Look at the computer screen. How realistic are the pictures? How many colors are available? Are the colors attractive? Does the computer language have special graphics commands and graphic symbols? These are a must to create any kind of still or animated picture.

Third, how about sound? Can the computer talk? If so, be sure to ask for a demonstration. The quality of computer speech synthesis varies dramatically. Some computers sound almost human, while others are barely intelligible. Does the computer come with a limited, canned vocabulary (such as TI's 99/4) or can you create your own words (as on Commodore's PET) using phonemes (speech sounds)?

Fourth, can the computer generate musical tones? Again, ask for a demonstration. What is the range of notes and chords? Can you compose your own music? Does the computer come with a music language?

Fifth, can you talk to the computer? If so, do it. Try to stump the computer. How slow must you talk? How limited is the computer's vocabulary?

Sixth, how about computer add-ons or attachments? Does the computer come with game paddles, a game console, or a keyboard? How about attachments that let you connect the computer to household appliances such as your stereo speakers or TV? Can your computer be hooked

Commodore's popular programmable PET computer, a device that uses phonemes, or speech sounds, to communicate with its operator.

up so it can talk on the telephone to other computers? Can it be plugged into a robot?

Seventh, how big is the computer? If it is very large, does it come on wheels? The Sharp computer is a general-purpose programmable model of today (you can program it in BASIC) that is so small, it can almost fit into your pocket.

Eighth, there's the speed and power of the computer to consider. What size CPU brain does the computer use, an older 8-bit brain or a newer and faster 16-bit brain? How about memory? Some of the newest small computers can store as much as half a million symbols (numbers and letters) in their online RAM memory.

How about backup memory? Does the computer use tape cassettes, floppy disks, hard disks, bubbles, or what? Tape cassettes are less expensive, but if you plan to build models and games on your computer, the newer kinds of memory will make them run much faster and be more realistic.

SUPERCOMPUTERS OF THE FUTURE

Computer brains once consisted of clanking pulleys, gnashing metal gears, and throbbing pistons powered by steam.

Then a new force, electricity, became the lifeblood of the computer brain. Inside the computer's thick steel skin, its brain hotly glowed from thousands of incandescent *vacuum tubes.* Its electrified information surged through miles of serpentine wires that overflowed from gray metal boxes.

Then came the cool, solid-state *transistor,* and inside the computer brain, the vacuum tubes disappeared and were replaced by stacks of transistor boards wired and soldered together. As their components multiplied, computer brains became prodigious, superfast, and baffling in their complexity.

But even now, as the computer's brain continues to grow, the individual parts within its brain—the tiny electronic circuits—are shrinking. Moreover, they are shrinking drastically. According to computer specialist Christopher Evans, "Thirty years ago a computer with the same number of functions as a human brain would have had to be the size of New York City and would have used more power than the subway system; today that computer would be the size of a TV set; in ten years, it will be as small as a human brain and will run on a transistor radio battery."

This incredible miniaturization will soon spawn new generations of midget supercomputers—machines that can store and digest billions of bits of information in a few trillionths of a second; machines that can operate at absolute zero (–273° C.); machines that can play brilliant, lifelike, fantasy adventure games with dozens of people—all at the same time.

The computer's appearance, too, is undergoing a revolution. Pick up a pencil, a keychain, a toothbrush, or a glass. In the near future, a computer might be hidden inside—a talking, listening, intelligent computer that might play a rock fugue for you while you write your grocery list, open the front door, brush your teeth, or sip some water.

Miniature computers will soon be everywhere yet invisible, gobbling up information and interacting with you in an almost humanlike manner. Whoever invented the gremlins, the leprechauns, the faeries, and all the other little people, had an insight into the future relationship between humans and this marvelous machine.

THE RISE OF JAPAN

At a recent international conference held in San Francisco, Japanese computer-chip manufacturers stunned their U.S. counterparts by announcing quarter-inch memory chips that stored 256,000 bits of data and "wafer memories" only three inches (7.5 cm) in diameter that stored over four million bits. U.S. companies have not yet even been able to produce a memory chip that can store 64,000 bits!

How can the Japanese squeeze so many bits onto their computer memories? The answer is that they have developed incredibly precise instruments of chip fabrication. For example U.S. instruments can now print a silicon-chip circuit that is 5 microns (5-millionths of a meter) wide. Yet Japanese instruments can print one that is only 1 micron wide.

How has Japanese technology become so advanced? In Japan, there is a combined government-industry push to make that nation the number one computer power of the 1980s. By 1985, the Japanese government, along with private investors, will have contributed over $70 billion to the computer industry. With this backing, Japan's technological progress can be expected to increase rapidly.

The U.S. government and computer industry will undoubtedly try to meet the Japanese challenge. But in the new few years it is the Japanese computer market we must look to, to see what amazing new computers emerge.

THE SHRINKING BRAIN

The first small-computer kit was introduced in early 1975. By today's standards, the kit was primitive, expensive, and relatively slow. Yet over the next few years, small computers will change even more.

The Supercomputers

The CPU, or central processing center, of a small computer is its brain. Computer CPUs are getting smaller, faster, and capable of handling more information. Notebook-sized small computers of the late 1980s will process tens of millions of instructions a second and access memories that will store more information than can be found in an entire encyclopedia. This kind of power will make small computers better at playing games, doing household chores, and helping you with your schoolwork. It will enable computers to communicate with you in your own language. And everyone in your family—or everyone in your class—will be able to use the small computer, all at the same time.

Most of the improvements in small computers will come from continued progress in miniaturizing the computer's wires—its *integrated circuits.* More circuits will fit on smaller chips. Scientists at Texas Instruments, for example, using a process called VLSI (*V*ery *L*arge *S*cale *I*ntegration), have managed to fit a million memory cells, or transistors, on a RAM chip less than ¼-inch square.

Thoughts That Fly

The decrease in chip size will have a dramatic effect on the speed of the computer circuits contained on the chip. When there are more circuits on a smaller area, there is less distance between each circuit; hence, it takes less time for the electrical signals to go from one part of the chip to another.

Due to "friction," or resistance, electrical signals approach—but do not match—the speed of light. Light travels so fast that it takes less than a second and a half to go from the earth to the moon. If an electrical signal inside a com-

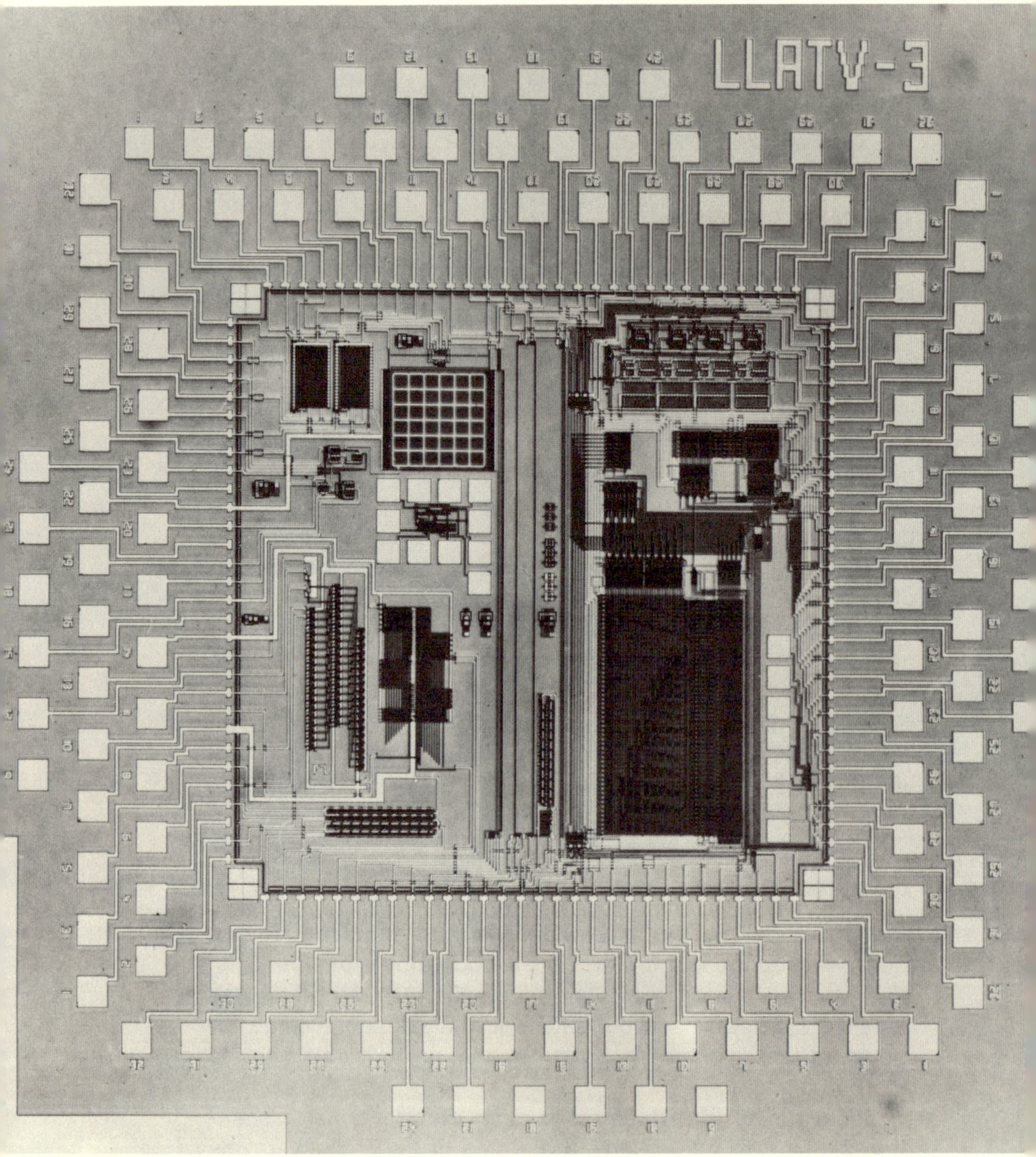
LLATV-3

puter met no resistance and could travel the speed of light, it would travel the length of a 3-foot (.9-m)-wide computer in only three-billionths of a second (or three *nanoseconds*).

"But that's still too slow!" claim the people who make the chips. "Let's cut down the number of signals that travel across the computer," they say. "Let's squeeze more of the computer onto a single chip." And they're doing it. By shrinking the distance signals have to travel, chip manufacturers are now making computers so fast, they're starting to achieve processing speeds of just a few *picoseconds* —a few trillionths of a second.

SMALL COMPUTERS THAT USE BIG WORDS

A bit is the basic unit of information inside a computer. A bit is either a "1" or a "0" and is represented by voltages that are high or low, on or off. When you group bits together, you create specially coded information—words, numbers, and commands for the computer to process.

The number of bits a computer's CPU can handle at a time is called its *word size.* The original computer chips in the 1960s and 1970s could process and store only two bits at a time—their words were only two bits long. Then came the 4-bit chips, then the 8-bit chips. Today, many small computers use 16-bit chips.* That is, today's small com-

* General-purpose (programmable) small computers use the 16-bit chips. The smaller videogame, hand-held, and appliance computers still use 4-bit and 8-bit chips.

An IBM logic chip illustrating VLSI—Very Large Scale Integration—of computer circuits.

A 16-bit CPU chip seen in relation to a pencil. This chip can handle information at more than double the speed of 8-bit chips and is much more powerful.

puters can handle a chunk of information—a word—that is sixteen bits long.

Small computers that use 16-bit CPUs should be at least twice as fast as the 8-bit machines, since they can store and process sixteen bits at a time, the 8-bit machine only eight. In fact, the 16-bit small computers are faster still. The reason is that they have a richer machine language built into their wires. While the 8-bit CPUs had instructions (or commands) that were eight, sixteen, or twenty-four bits long, the 16-bit CPUs have instructions of up to forty-eight bits. With more bits, the instructions are more powerful. A single 16-bit instruction might do as much as four 8-bit instructions. This makes the 16-bit computer faster. For example, the average 8-bit computer can do about four thousand subtraction problems (such as 561 – 239 = 322) in a single second. But the fastest 16-bit small computers can do almost twenty times as many.

Besides being fast, the 16-bit CPU chips can store huge amounts of memory. Current 8-bit CPUs are limited to sixty-four thousand bytes of main memory. Current 16-bit machines have over two hundred times that amount.

What will the future bring? Chip manufacturers have already announced 32-bit chips, with 64-bit chips to follow soon after. Eventually computer brains that can handle words of up to 256 bits will appear, possibly in the next ten to twenty years.

How big an English word is a computer word of 256 bits? Since it takes eight bits to make a letter from the alphabet, the small computer of the future will be able to handle English words of up to thirty-two letters at a time. Picture the small computer at a spelling contest:

Judge: *Computer, spell the word that describes the group of people in England at the time of Henry VIII who were against removing Roman Catholicism as the country's official religion.*

Computer: *(A millionth of a second later)*
A-N-T-I-D-I-S-E-S-T-A-B-L-I-S-H-M-E-N-T-A-R-I-A-N-I-S-T-S.
Antidisestablishmentarianists.
(A breeze—only twenty-nine letters.)

THE FROZEN COMPUTER

Computers based on silicon chips are going to be smaller and faster and will hold more memory. But silicon chips are approaching their limit in terms of speed and size. Clearly, if computers are going to keep improving, a new technology is needed. Is there such a technology? There are, in fact, many technologies currently being developed. One of the most promising—and fascinating—involves the *Josephson Junction computer,* a computer design based on a discovery by the scientist Brian Josephson in 1962.

Electrons conduct electricity, and electricity powers the small computer. Unfortunately, as electrons flow across the semiconductor material in a computer chip, they encounter an energy barrier that reduces their speed. But Josephson discovered a *tunnel junction* that gives electrons the energy to overcome this barrier. As a result, Josephson circuits lose less energy in the form of heat, require less power to operate, can be packed onto incredibly dense chips, and are extraordinarily fast. Computers based on Josephson circuits are capable of operating in as little as thirteen trillionths of a second. This is up to a hundred times faster than today's fastest semiconductor-circuit computers.

But this unimaginable swiftness doesn't come easily. The flow of electrons—the current—depends on the amount of friction the electrons encounter in a wire or circuit. A wire with little friction is said to be *conductive.* One way to make any wire more conductive is to reduce its temperature. To enable electrons to overcome the energy barrier in Josephson circuits, the wires are immersed in liquid helium and supercooled at 459° F. below zero. That's only four degrees above absolute zero. At this extremely low temperature, the tiny circuits become *superconductive,* losing almost all resistance to the flow of electric current.

In addition, the manufactured junction circuits must be less than a millionth of a centimeter thick. That's so small that the thickness of the barriers is measured in *atoms!*

In spite of these hurdles, Josephson computers already exist. By the late 1980s or early 1990s, many small computers will come equipped with one of these supercooled, superfast brains. These machines will be so fast and so

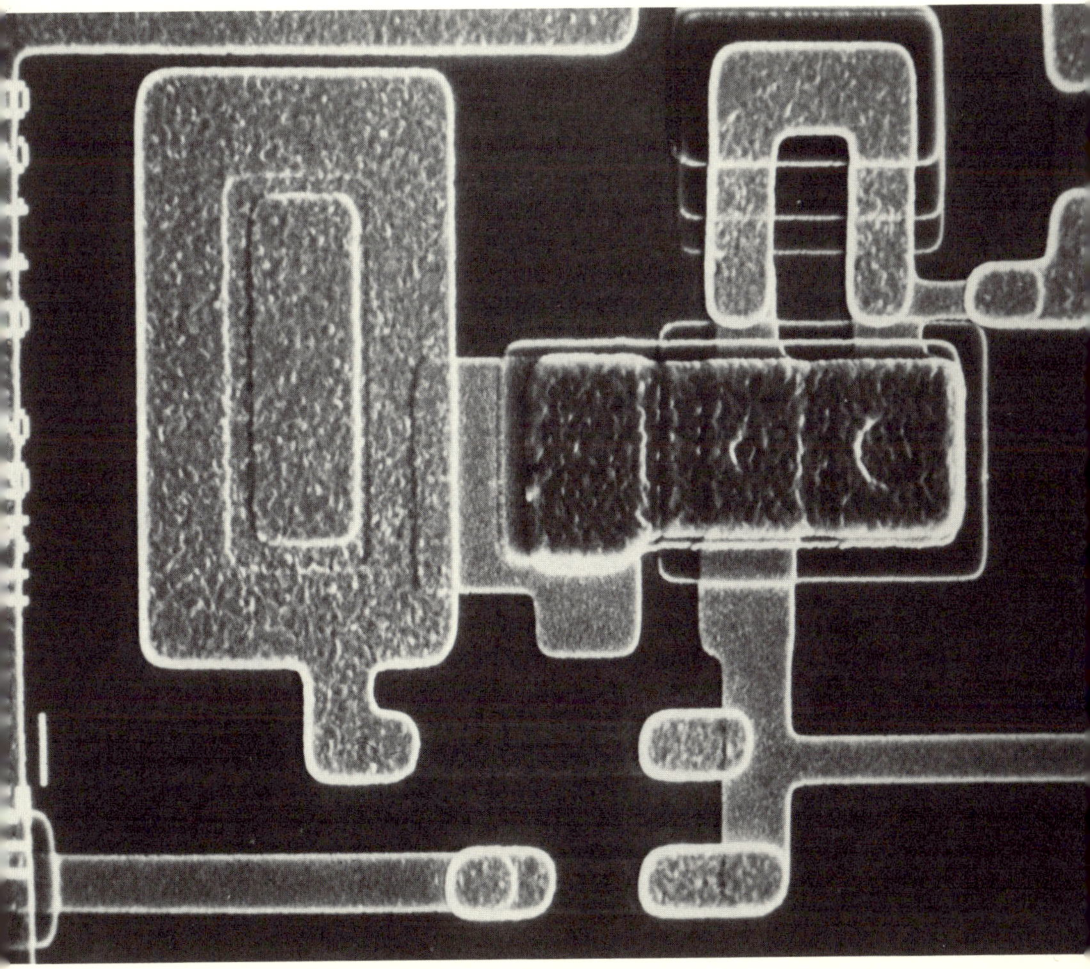

A highly magnified Josephson (tunnel) junction, seen here on an IBM chip. Josephson junction computers will have ultrafast computer "brains" that will operate at near-absolute zero temperatures.

powerful, they will be able to run circles around some of the most sophisticated computers operating today.

TWO HEADS ARE BETTER

One way to make faster, more powerful computers is to invent smaller and faster computer circuits. Another way is to design computers differently. The way a small computer is designed now, it has one CPU that runs one machine-language instruction at a time—just one. On computers of the future, things will be quite different. New designs will enable a computer to process several commands or pieces of data (or both) at the same time—a parallel computer.

In the future CPU chips, in addition to being smaller, will be less expensive. This will enable small computers to be designed as *multiprocessor* devices—computers with several CPUs. If, for example, a small computer has six CPUs wired together, then it can process six different instructions at the same time.

In today's small computer, the CPU handles only one instruction or piece of data at a time. Small computers of the future are more likely to operate as *pipeline processors* —assembly lines of data and instructions.

What happens if you combine a pipeline small computer with a parallel small computer? You get an *array small computer.* An array is like a table, full of neat little columns and rows of boxes. In an array computer, each box would be a separate CPU chip.

A LOT ON ITS MIND

Sometime in the near future you might be able to sit down at your small computer and do a math problem in a few nanoseconds, then store the answer in a computer memory capable of holding millions of bits of information. But what difference does it make to you if the computer solves the problem in a thousandth of a second or a billionth of a second—especially since it takes you fifteen seconds just to type the problem into the computer? And where would you ever find enough information to fill up so much computer memory?

You probably couldn't. The small computer of the future will have too much processing power for just one person. But it will be perfect for letting several people all use it at the same time. When a computer works for several users at once, it is called a *multiprogrammed time-sharing system*—multiprogrammed because its memory is divided up into partitions (space for several different programs and their data) and time-shared because each second of the computer's time is shared with many users.

Picture an evening at home in the future. You're doing a science project, your younger sister is having a story read to her, your father is working on a floor plan for an addition to your house, and your mom, an attorney, is preparing a brief for a case she will argue in court the next day. What would you all have in common? You would all be using the small computer. It would be helping you for a fraction of a second, turning its attention to your sister for another fraction, moving on to your mom and dad for a couple of more fractions, then, before you've noticed, be back helping you again. And it would still have enough brainpower left over to run the burglar alarm and the smoke alarm, monitor the phone, record a movie you're missing on TV, keep an eye on the entire household's temperature and humidity, and feed instructions to the robot maid busy vacuuming the living room—all at the same time. And it's working so fast that it seems to you as if you have the computer all to yourself.

A MEMORY LIKE AN ELEPHANT

Even today, a small computer operates at blinding speed. But not all parts within the computer operate at the same speed. A small computer's semiconductor memory—ROM and RAM—and its brain, or CPU, are incredibly fast. Yet the computer's printer and video terminal (picture screen and keyboard) are thousands of times slower. The mass or removable memory, like the tape cassettes and floppy disks, are also much slower. For example, it takes as little as one ten-millionth of a second to access a bit stored on semiconductor RAM memory, while it takes a second or more on a floppy disk and a minute or more on a tape cassette.

But technology is advancing rapidly here, too. It is likely that small computers of the future will use disks as opposed to tapes. Disks will cost less, will hold more information, and will operate far faster. But the disks will not look like today's floppy. Instead they will be rigid and mounted permanently inside the disk drive attached to the computer. They will store one hundred times as much information as a floppy and be ten times as fast. The new disks, or *platters,* will be highly polished with a tough, glassy finish. Although they will resist such bugaboos as fingerprints and oxide from the air, they will still have an Achilles heel. If even one drop of saliva gets on them, they will be ruined. And, according to one hard-disk manufacturer, "Yawns are killers." (The moisture in people's breath adheres to the surface of the disk and damages it.)

CCD Chips for Your Pictures

Disks—hard and soft—will be around for a while, but there are already challengers entering the ring. One of these is the *CCD* (the *C*harge-*C*oupled *D*evice). CCD storage cells, storing a bit each, are even smaller than RAM cells. This allows CCD circuits to be packed even more densely than RAM. Already CCD chips have been fabricated that can store 64,000 bits, and chips with twice that storage capacity are predicted in the near future.

But unlike RAM or disk memory, CCD memory is serial. This means that when the CPU goes to fetch a byte of information from CCD, it can't go right to the byte it wants. Instead, it has to scan several bytes until it finds the correct one. This makes CCD slower than RAM but still much faster than either disk or tape. An ideal use for CCD will be as memory for a programmable computer's picture screen. CCD's quickness and large storage capacity will enable the computer user to produce realistic models and animated color movies.

Bubble Memory

Another technology in its early stages is based on *mobile magnetic bubbles,* bubbles that can be grouped together on a chip even more compact than a CCD. Bubble memory was first developed in 1967 by Andrew Bobeck of Bell Telephone Laboratories. It is produced by placing a thin magnetic film on a nonmagnetic surface such as garnet. A magnetic bubble forms when a magnetic field is generated around the film by two permanent magnets. A coil of wire is wrapped around the bubble device. When current is passed through the coil, the bubbles move.

Each bubble can carry a bit of data. Up to ten million bubbles have already been squeezed onto a single chip. What's more, a bubble memory behaves like both ROM and RAM. Like RAM, information can be stored and retrieved; like ROM, the information is not erased when the power is turned off. It is likely that bubble memory will eventually replace disk memory on small computers.

Bubble technology is developing rapidly. Scientists at Bell Laboratories have developed a way to replace the bubble drive's relatively bulky and slow electric coils with wafer-thin layers of gold or aluminum. The new bubble memories are cheaper, run ten times faster, and are four times smaller. However, bubbles are still not competitive with RAM since, like CCD, they store information serially and are therefore slower.*

MASKED KEYBOARDS AND SKINNY SCREENS

The keyboard is the chief way to enter information or commands into the small computer. In the future, the keyboard on small computers will come with several sets of plastic key *masks* that will fit over the original keys. Each mask will be for use with a different program and different computer language. There will be masks that let you type in moves for a game; masks that have graphic characters for drawing pictures; foreign-language masks with special letters and symbols; text-editor masks for when you want to write and edit book reports, research papers, letters, and so on; and masks with musical symbols to let you copy or compose your own music.

* RAM technology is spurting forward, too. Scientists at Hughes Aircraft Corporation have invented a new kind of RAM called NOVRAM that, like bubble memory, retains its information even when the computer is turned off.

Printers and Plotters

Almost all small computers of the future are likely to come with a printer and a plotter. You'll use the printer to type out reports, letters, shopping lists, answers to your homework—anything using letters or words. You'll use the plotter to draw pictures, diagrams, graphs, maps, and figures.

Picture Screens

Most small-computer picture screens today are really just television sets, black and white or color. Screens in the future will be radically different. There will be plasma-ray screens, Liquid Crystal Displays (LCDs—like you see on a wristwatch), and large-scale "movie theatre" screens. They will be thin and flat and offer an extremely sharp and realistic picture, composed of a million or more pixels—picture elements—per screen.

CAMERAS, LIGHT PENS, AND COPYCATS

In the future typewriterlike keyboards, even with masks, will be far less important as a means for issuing commands or entering information into the computer. You will use other devices instead, each one suited to a particular purpose. For example, to enter music into the computer, you will use keys that look like those on an organ or a piano. Dozens of microphones hidden behind walls and hooked into an intercom will enable you to talk to the computer from anywhere in your home or classroom. Cameras will pick up visual images and relay them to the computer. And you will have fancy "joy sticks" and game consoles for playing games.

The *light pen* is another device that will come with the small computer of the future. By pointing a light pen at the computer's screen, you will be able to select from a program or information menu, draw or paint pictures, select musical notes for a song you are composing, construct molecule chains for chemistry class, or draw circles, squares, triangles, and trapezoids for your geometry class.

Light pens will also let you create complex building

blocks—graphic symbols—of bricks, steel beams, arteries, atoms, wires, or bones. You can use the symbols to copy other designs or to create designs of your own—designs for buildings, bridges, new computers, even new life forms.

Another device that will commonly be found on small computers of the future is the *digitizer.* You'll use a digitizer to copy two-dimensional shapes (maps, faces, etc.) into the computer's memory.

The Copycat is one type of digitizer. Using a single wheel, it moves around on a square plastic grid. Its location on the grid is translated into a digital address that is stored in the computer's memory.

THE TALKING, SINGING COMPUTER

Already small computers by the hundreds can talk and listen and play music. But their talent is still limited. For them to understand your voice, you must talk slowly and distinctly, one word at a time. Their voices are getting more humanlike, but they still sound like machines. And their music is composed of simple tones, not the full, rich music produced by a musical instrument.

What makes small computers unable to master sound? The major problem is that today's small computers lack the speed and memory needed to capture the "timbre" frequencies of a sound wave. And it is timbre that gives a voice or musical instrument its own unique tone, or sound. Instead the computer captures samples, or "slices," of the sound waves, digitizes them (by translating them into ones and zeros), then stores and reproduces them. The resulting sounds are not as full and rich as those produced by the large computers used in professional recording studios.

In the near future small computers will have the speed and memory to capture and reproduce all the characteristics of a sound wave, including timbre. These small computers will operate in billionths of a second and will store millions of pieces of information in their main memory. They will accurately reproduce your voice, a middle C on a piano, a chord strummed on a guitar, or a three-part harmony sung by a vocal group.

1979 U.S. POPULATION DENSITIES

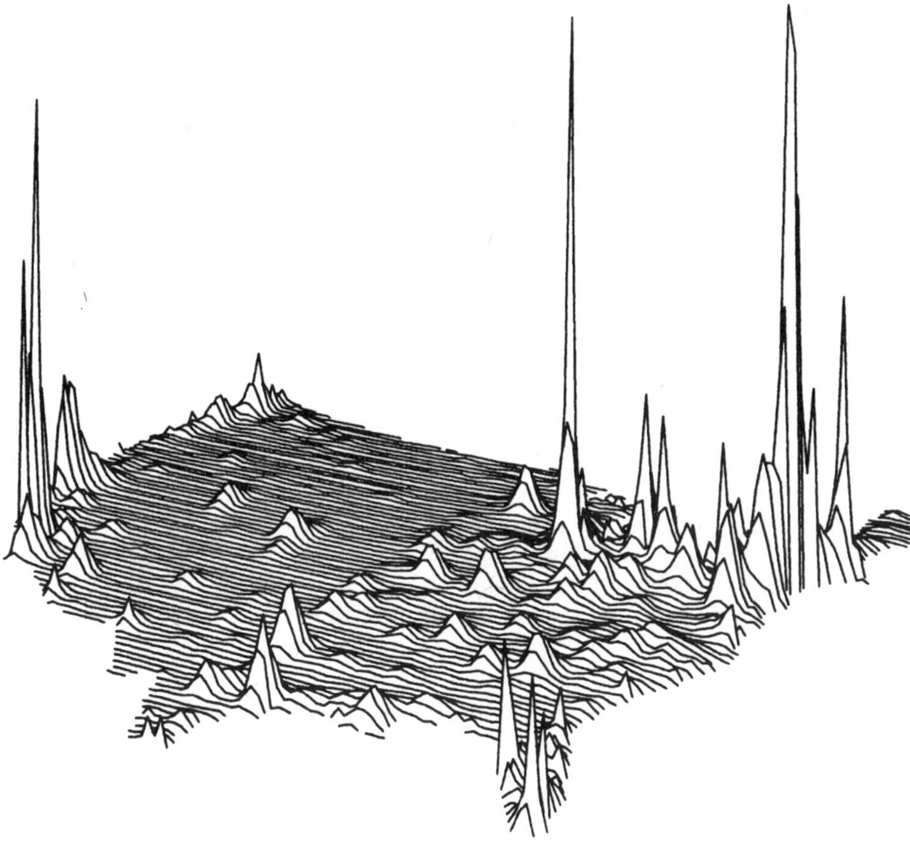

Produced by Aspex Program
Harvard Laboratory for Computer Graphics & Spatial Analysis

Data for 1970 and 1979 estimates of population, by county, supplied by the National Planning Data Corporation, Ithaca, New York

Surrounded by Voices

The small computer's ability to talk and listen and play music will make it into an exciting game machine and an effective electronic tutor. But even the smallest special-purpose computers in the future will have an advanced mastery over sound in comparison to today's computers. And, remember, due to their size, these computers can be hidden inside almost any other object, machine, or appliance. Thus, you are soon likely to see—and hear!—thermometers that tell you your temperature or advise you that it's going to be cold when you step outside the house; cars that tell you when they are overheating or their fuel is low; ovens that tell you when your meal is cooked; containers that inform you of the quantity of liquid they are holding; "intelligent" typewriters that automatically correct your spelling errors and conduct impromptu "spelling bees" whenever you misspell a word; wood furniture that complains when there is too much or too little moisture in the air; refrigerators that nag you to throw away leftovers; and doorbells and telephones that sing instead of ring.

Help for the Handicapped—and the Absentminded

Think how a room with talking computers could help a person who is feeble, bedridden, or blind. If the person wanted to write a letter but couldn't, no matter. He or she could dictate the letter to a typewriter, which would then mail the letter electronically. To make a telephone call, the person could ask the phone to look up the number and make the call. Then he or she could have a conversation without

A computer graphics map of U.S. population densities in 1979, created by the Harvard Laboratory for Computer Graphics & Spatial Analysis. By creating your own computer graphics you will be able to learn concepts such as this one in new and exciting ways.

ever getting up from bed. To find out the time or set an alarm, the person could just ask the clock.

There is also relief in sight for those of us who are absentminded or maybe just nearsighted. Suppose when you get up in the morning, you can never remember where you left your eyeglasses before you went to bed. You can't find them on the bedside table. They're not on the bookshelf beside the bed. Nor are they on the floor. Where are they?

In the future your eyeglasses might have a computer inside. You will be able to softly call out, "Glasses. Where are you?" And the glasses, tucked inside your T-shirt and midway down inside the clothes hamper in the closet, will reply, "Here I am . . . Here I am . . . Here I am . . ."

The Wristcomputer

In the future the computer's improved ability to replicate and to understand human speech will make it possible for it to communicate with you almost entirely on a verbal basis. This development will make a lot of people more comfortable dealing with computers. Also, since it will no longer be necessary to include a finger-sized keypad along with a computer, ultrasmall computers that talk, sing, and listen will become commonplace. For example take the wristcomputer that, responding to a verbal request from you, might tell you the time, give you a phone number you need, play your favorite song, unlock your electronically locked front door, ask you a riddle, tell you a joke, play a game, compute the number of weeks it will take you to save up for a new speaker for your stereo, or remind you that you're supposed to be home for dinner at six.

Martha's Talking Door

What will a home security system of the future be like? Let's take the case of Martha B., an elderly widow living alone in a city apartment. The door to Martha's apartment has a tiny computer embedded inside it. Whenever anyone knocks on the door, the computer—in a strong, authoritative voice—asks, "Who is it, please?" When the person answers, the computer relays the visitor's answer to Martha and, at the same time, performs a search of all the "friendly" voices it has stored in its memory. If a match for the person's voice is not found, the computer asks, "State your business, please." If anything suspicious occurs—for example, if the person doesn't answer—the computer automatically sounds an alarm, warns Martha, fastens additional locks on the door, and calls the police, the building superintendent, and several of Martha's friends and relatives.

Want to Sing like Stevie Wonder? Play like J. S. Bach?

Musical computers of the future will encourage you to be creative and give you great personal satisfaction. For example, say you love to sing, but when you try to belt out a tune, you end up croaking like a frog. No problem. In the near future computerized voice enhancers will become available that will enable you to sing into a microphone and have the song come out of your speakers as a song sung by Stevie Wonder, the Bee Gees, the Mormon Tabernacle Choir, or anyone else you choose. A little further into the future, if you are not satisfied with the voice you have (singing or otherwise), you will be able to go into the hospital and have a miniature voice enhancer surgically implanted inside your throat. For your new voice, you will be able to have any voice you choose—someone else's or something completely new.

And how about your desire to play a musical instrument? Soon, you will be able to sit down at a small computer or a computerized music machine. Knowing only a few notes, you will be able to compose a simple song. The computer will take over and ask you: COMPOSER? You will reply, "JS Bach." The computer will ask, "INSTRUMENT?" You'll think a moment, then answer, "Pipe organ." (You

Over: using future versions of this "musical" Atari 400 computer you will be able to compose your own music (and then listen to it) in only a short time and with very little musical training.

PHRASE 1 2035
MEASURE 1 FREE
SMI, NOTE?
ATARI 400

could just as well have answered "harmonica" or "orchestra.")

A fraction of a second later, the computer will begin playing your song over its stereo speakers. Is it still the simple, monophonic ditty you composed? No longer. Now it has been embellished with the chords, the meter, the tempo, and the dynamics characteristic of Bach. And it sounds like it's being played on a full-size pipe organ, the kind you might find in a German cathedral.

COMPUTER LANGUAGES OF THE FUTURE

How do computers talk? How do computers sing? How do computers do anything? They do it with electricity, pulses and charges of electricity that race along the computer's wires at fantastic speeds.

When the first electrically powered computers were invented back in the 1930s and 1940s, it was discovered that the most efficient way to code information inside the computer was using two-state, or binary, logic—either ON or OFF. If an electrical charge were high or just plain present, a binary one was being represented. If an electrical charge were low or not there at all, that circuit registered a binary zero. In the early days of computers, all information that people wanted to feed the computer had to be manually converted into binary ones and zeros and "toggled" or "wired" into the computer using special switches and detachable wires. Complex mathematical formulas and millions of numbers had to be translated into strings of ones and zeros and then back again.

After years of struggling through manual translation, people finally realized the computer could do the translation itself. Computer programs could be written using commands that resembled English. Then the computer could translate these commands back into the ones and zeros, the high and low electrical charges that it could store and process.

The view of the computer as its own translator stimulated computer scientists to develop newer and more powerful languages. Some languages were special-purpose and were really useful only for certain jobs such as medical diagnosis, military ballistics, and statistical analysis. Other languages were general-purpose and attempted to convey the full power of the computer to the programmer and user. Still others were natural languages that tried to approximate human speech and language and thereby make computers accessible to everyone.

In the years ahead computer languages will evolve even faster to keep up with the vastly expanded speed and storage capabilities of future computers. At present, small computers are still limited by their size to simple, relatively primitive languages such as BASIC. In the future, these computers will have the memory and speed to handle almost any language that is developed.

Already today there are some new languages being developed that are easy to use and that show great promise as powerful small computer languages of tomorrow. One of these languages is SMALLTALK, developed by the Xerox Corporation in Palo Alto, California. SMALLTALK lends itself to managing, organizing, and retrieving large quantities of information and to producing attractive visual images quickly. This last feature will make it simple for anyone to build colorful, animated computer models. SMALLTALK will be discussed in greater detail in a later section.

SMALLTALK and other languages such as LOGO (developed at the Artificial Intelligence Lab at MIT in Cambridge, Massachusetts), will also make it easier for nonprogrammers to learn programming.* They will become the primary impetus behind a new group of "electronic tutors" that may revolutionize the way young people learn. Tools provided by the languages will enable students to take unstimulating or difficult concepts and translate them into realistic musical or visual models. With these languages the person will learn faster and more efficiently. Learning will become more self-directed and original. Young people trained on computers and fluent in computer languages are likely to develop awesome intelligence. They will become so adept at model building and at interconnecting and manipulating theories, concepts, and principles of nature that they will produce a flood of new discoveries and inventions that could quickly alter the very fabric of society.

---

* See section four for more information on LOGO.

EVOLUTION OF COMPUTER LANGUAGES

All of a computer's information and commands are coded in machine language—long strings of ones and zeros representing electrical charges inside the computer. When the first computers were built, people communicated with them in machine language, the computer's own tongue. But people soon got tired of flicking switches and trying to keep all of the computer's ones and zeros straight. Since the computer was a natural translator, they reasoned, why not let the computer translate people's commands into machine language, and vice versa? They tried it, it worked, and the first translator programs were born. First came the assemblers (such as BAL and SAP), next the compilers (such as FORTRAN and COBOL), and finally the interpreters (such as BASIC and APL). These programs, developed largely in the 1950s and early 1960s, are now in use on almost every computer in the world.

Yet even after the development of the translator programs, people still were not satisfied. Translator programs still required a special language, some code other than English. And there were those who wanted to free humans from any translation at all. They set out to produce higher-level compilers and interpreters that would enable people to talk to computers in a natural language such as English.

Also, there were people who felt that even the compilers and interpreters were too complicated, too ambitious, or not sufficiently structured. Some of these people set out to devise special-purpose languages that could be used for gaming, simulation, planning, economics, and business. Others set out to devise rigorous, tightly organized languages that would help people to write programs that were straightforward and free from *bugs,* or errors.

By the late 1970s, dozens of new languages had been invented. The new languages were described as "high level" since they often resembled English. They were abstract and able to do many operations based on just a single command. These languages were powerful, easy to use, and popular.

The ongoing miniaturization of electronic circuits, the development of new ways to process information, and the invention of new technologies such as the Josephson Junction will soon make it possible to develop languages that are even more English-like, more abstract, and more powerful. The work on new very high-level languages and even ultrahigh level languages has, in fact, already begun.

What will these future languages be like? There will be three main types: natural languages that will resemble a spoken and written language such as English; special-purpose languages that will enable you to do something very specific such as draw pictures, compose music, or manage millions of bits of information; and problem-solving languages that will give you the tools to logically and accurately solve a wide variety of problems.

WHY NOT USE ENGLISH?

Suppose you've decided to learn how to program small computers. Why won't you just use English? After all, you already know English, and the smart, fast computers of the future will, too.

It's true that English—and all other "natural," or human, languages—serves as an excellent way for people to converse and learn general concepts. But languages of this sort often are unsuitable for more advanced kinds of thinking such as logical or scientific thinking. Because they are so limited, people have already developed alternative languages, including mathematics. These and other artificial languages have new vocabularies and symbols that encourage more sophisticated thinking.

With the help of some of the greatest human minds and using alternate languages, we have gradually come to know more about ourselves and the world around us. These ideas are embodied in design concepts, complicated ideas that describe how things are built and how they work—how atoms can be split to release energy, how spaceships operate in outer space, how surgery may be performed on the retina of the eye; how light, shadow, and perspective can be reflected on the two-dimensional surface of a painting; how to capture the greatest human emotions in modulated waves of sound—otherwise known as music. Once discovered, these design concepts can be learned and employed more easily if they are expressed in a special-purpose artificial language such as musical notation or calculus.

In addition, it often pays to use an artificial language simply because of the shortcuts that language offers. For example, if you were doing homework for a statistics course, would you prefer to express a problem you had to write this way?

Ten times nine times eight times seven times six times five times four times three times two times one

This way?

$$10 \times 9 \times 8 \times 7 \times 6 \times 5 \times 4 \times 3 \times 2 \times 1$$

Or this way?

$$10!\ ^{*}$$

On the other hand, there are many simple functions a computer can do at home or at school that don't require an artificial language. In these cases, English will do fine. In the future, then, there will be English-like languages as well as special-purpose languages and problem-solving languages. Your computer won't speak just one of these; it will speak many languages equally well. Like an interpreter working for the United Nations, the computer will be able to shift quickly and smoothly from one language to the next.

SMALLTALK

Why have several languages for tomorrow's small computers? Why not have a single language that can handle almost any project you dream up? That's the goal of the Learning Research Group, a team of educators and computer spe-

---

* You read this as "ten-factorial." It means take ten and multiply it by nine; then take the product and multiply it by eight; take the product and multiply it by seven; and so on until you get to one.

cialists at Xerox Corporation's Palo Alto Research Center (PARC) in California.

The team started its project some years ago by trying to estimate how advanced small computers would be in the middle or late 1980s. Then they built a computer that was larger but could perform the same tasks as the small computer you'll soon have in your classroom or home.

After several years of research, and with the advice of hundreds of visitors, including young people, teachers, artists, musicians, and scientists, the team developed a language and programming system known as SMALLTALK. SMALLTALK is a powerful tool for solving problems and for doing specialized tasks such as managing large files of information or creating computer games, experiments, and "movies."

The Dynabook

SMALLTALK's computer is called the Dynabook. At present the Dynabook is a "desktop" computer, weighing about as much as a medium-sized TV. But by the mid-1980s, it will be the size of a notebook. It will have at least a quarter-million bytes of memory, a flat, high-resolution picture screen, a typewriter keyboard, and a pointing device, currently known as a "mouse."

When you turn Dynabook on, it will flash a "menu" of options on the screen. You will be able to select one of these options by pointing at it with your finger (the screen will respond to your touch) or with the mouse pointer. Using SMALLTALK, you will be able to program the Dynabook to make music and "talk." The main Dynabook memory will be supported by an enormous backup memory of millions of bytes. Also, a Dynabook will be able to communicate with other Dynabooks and with a larger, central computer. The Dynabooks will be able to share information with each other and will use the main computer the way you might use a library—as a vast storehouse of available knowledge. The Dynabooks will be able to "check out" (retrieve) information from the main computer and instantly display it in the form of a pie chart, a table of numbers, an animated cartoon, or a page of text.

Classes and Objects

SMALLTALK is unusual because it is both a programming language and an operating system to control the Dynabook computer. Yet that's not the only reason SMALLTALK is so different from the majority of today's small-computer languages. To better understand how different SMALLTALK really is, let's first review how current programming languages work, then contrast them with SMALLTALK.

When you write a program using the current programming languages, you use two basic concepts—*data* and *algorithms.* The algorithm is the plan or method the program uses to reshape, or process, the data. In other words, an algorithm is like a recipe, and the data corresponds to the ingredients called for in the recipe.

This approach, though it is universally used and does work, has two major problems. First, it results in the computer being able to work on only one activity at a time. Second, as tasks and projects become more complex, writing programs that are error-free becomes more and more difficult.

SMALLTALK is very different. According to Alan Kay, one of SMALLTALK's chief designers, "Instead of manipulating inert ingredients with recipes, SMALLTALK's programs proceed like stage directions or football plays that coordinate active, independent players."

SMALLTALK still uses algorithms and data. But it also adds new concepts known as *classes, objects,* and *messages.* Kay's players are SMALLTALK's objects. What characteristics does an object have? First, it has memory; it can remember. Second, an object can communicate with other objects by sending messages. Third, if an object receives a message it understands, it can respond either by sending one or more messages or by changing itself.

Everything in a SMALLTALK program is an object. If you were to create a large number of objects, it might be difficult to tell them apart. To help you keep things straight, SMALLTALK allows you to group similar objects together into classes. An object belongs to the same class as another object if it responds to the same messages and has the same memory requirements.

A SMALLTALK Play

Hundreds of young people have visited the Xerox facility in Palo Alto and have learned to program in SMALLTALK. The SMALLTALK designers compare writing a SMALLTALK program to directing a movie or a play. The actors and actresses in the play are the SMALLTALK objects. As you write your program, you can give each object a personality (the messages each object sends and receives), an action (the object's so-called "changes of state"—its different colors, sizes, locations on the screen, and so on), and a past (the object's memory). Most important of all, you can give the objects—the players—physical form. You can draw them on the screen using the mouse or make the player's physical description part of the object itself. When you are ready for your play to begin, you send the object the message SHOW, and your first player appears on the computer picture screen.

Parallel Processing

If you were writing a SMALLTALK program (play) you could create objects with any number of physical forms. This is one of SMALLTALK's strongpoints. Using relatively few commands, you could have your object perform any number of actions. To do the same thing in most other small-computer languages would take dozens, maybe even hundreds, of commands.

In addition, SMALLTALK has the ability to handle more than one object at the same time. According to one computer expert, the objects in SMALLTALK are like a network of small computers all operating simultaneously.

To put it another way, if you really did create, say, a hundred different objects for your play, you would be using SMALLTALK to divide your computer into a hundred different tiny computers, each obeying a different set of commands. This illusion of simultaneous processing of program commands—of one hundred computers instead of just one—is known as *parallel processing.* It is closer to the way your own mind works.

Think about it. Your brain almost never focuses on one

thing at a time. To take an example, in a single instant you might be using your brain to chew a chocolate bar, watch a beautiful sunset, walk down a street, breathe, digest the candy bar, hear and smell a city bus, and worry about the tooth that's bothering you!

This kind of parallel processing is normal and necessary. Real life requires the brain to handle many things being thrown at it at the same time. That's why the brain is programmed to simultaneously process information coming from several directions at once. Using SMALLTALK, you'll be able to program your computer the same way.

From Simple to Complex

SMALLTALK objects can be as simple as a rectangle or as complex as buildings, electronics diagrams, models of the U.S. economy, and animated cartoons with sound effects.

How do you create the more complex objects? By first creating simple objects and then using those objects as building blocks to create more complicated objects. And you do not have to remember, as you are building, how all the simple objects underneath work. It's very much like a large organization. When the president of a large corporation gives an order, he or she doesn't need to worry about how each employee does the job. What matters is that the job gets done. And that's how large, complex objects work in SMALLTALK.

ROSETTA

As remarkable as SMALLTALK is, the Learning Research Group at Xerox is working to improve it even further. SMALLTALK—as a language and as a programming system —will keep evolving until the development of a real note-

ROSETTA, an already-available form of SMALLTALK, makes using the computer more practical as well as more exciting.

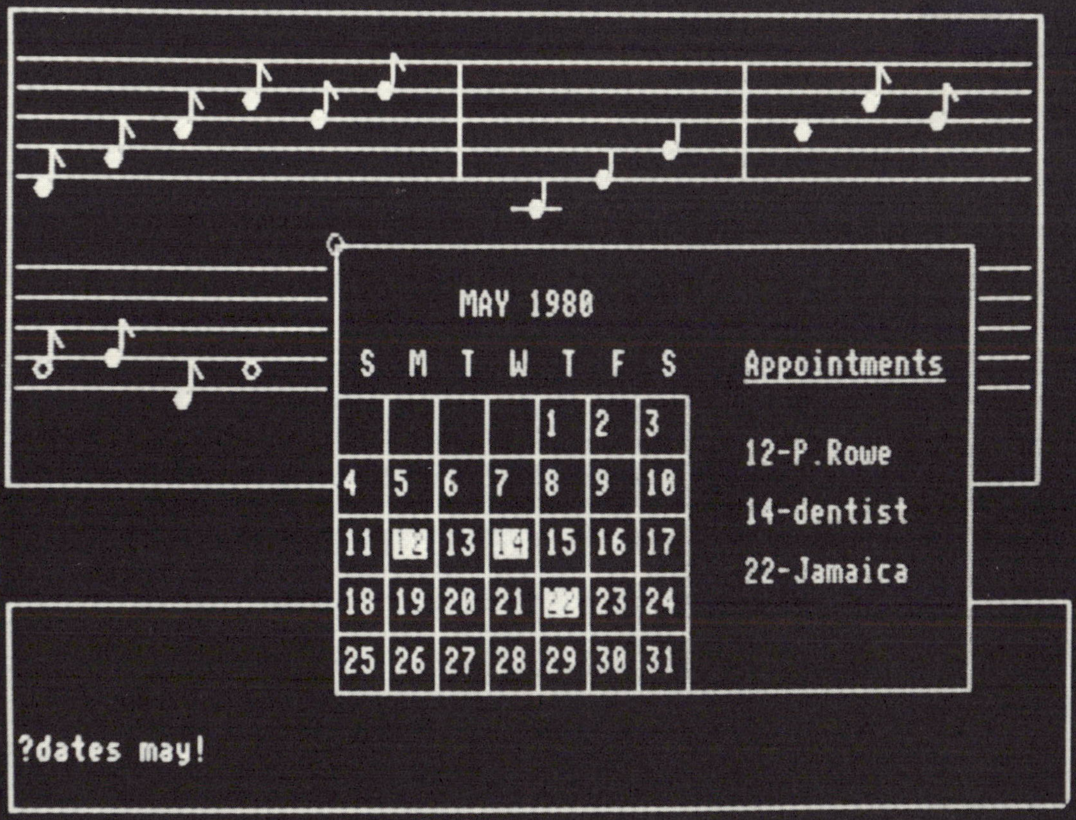

MAY 1980
S M T W T F S
1 2 3
4 5 6 7 8 9 10
11 12 13 14 15 16 17
18 19 20 21 22 23 24
25 26 27 28 29 30 31
Appointments
12-P.Rowe
14-dentist
22-Jamaica
?dates may!

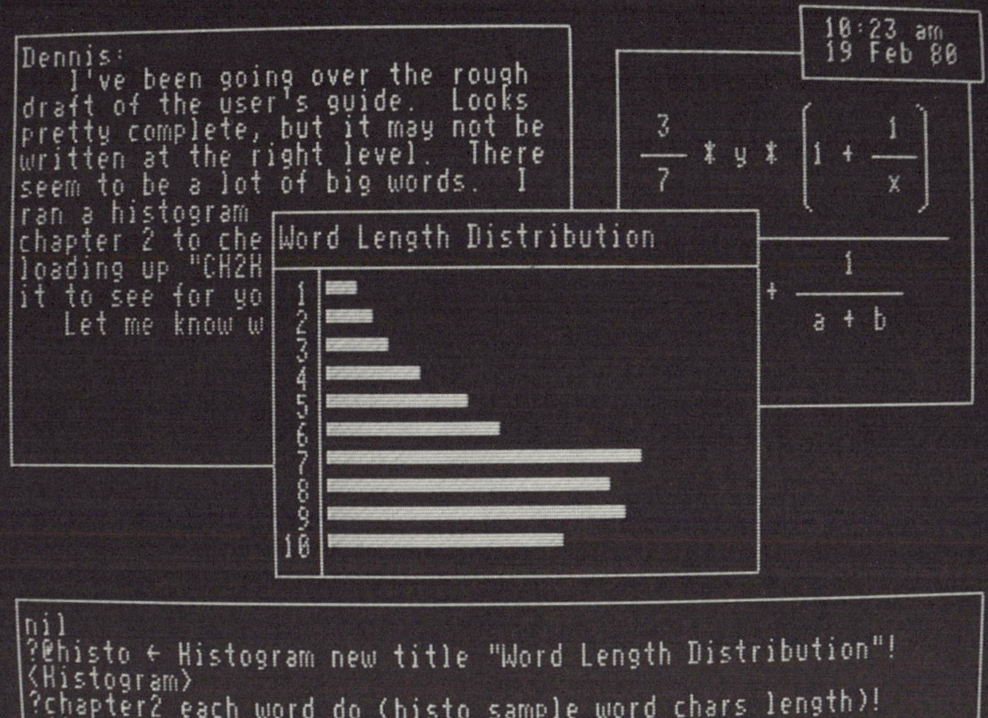

10:23 am
19 Feb 80
Dennis:
I've been going over the rough
draft of the user's guide. Looks
pretty complete, but it may not be
written at the right level. There
seem to be a lot of big words. I
ran a histogram
chapter 2 to che
loading up "CH2H
it to see for yo
Let me know w
Word Length Distribution
1
2
3
4
5
6
7
8
9
10
nil
?@histo ← Histogram new title "Word Length Distribution"!
<Histogram>
?chapter2 each word do (histo sample word chars length)!
nil
?_

book-sized Dynabook computer, and maybe afterward as well.

By the time you read this book, a complete Dynabook computer may still be unavailable. On the other hand, scaled-down versions of SMALLTALK are already starting to appear, and these versions—with names such as ROSETTA and TINYTALK—will run on today's small computers.

ROSETTA, for example, is offered by Rosetta, Inc. (named after the Rosetta stone that provided the key to Egyptian hieroglyphics). ROSETTA is similar to an early (1972) version of SMALLTALK. It doesn't run as fast, the graphics are not nearly as sophisticated, and it doesn't have many of the Dynabook's exciting features (including voice and music output, the "digitizer" mouse, etc.).

On the other hand, ROSETTA shares some of SMALLTALK's most important qualities, which makes it an unusually powerful small-computer language. For example, using ROSETTA on a current small computer, you can write short, simple programs that will manage your personal information, build computer models, create exciting games, solve problems, and design new conceptual tools. Designing new tools is also known as *language extensibility.* It means you can use ROSETTA commands (objects and messages) to design your own new commands.

You build new commands the way you build new objects in SMALLTALK. You start by combining simple building blocks. Eventually you wind up with a command that is powerful and complex. And since you designed it yourself, it is also unique.

ROBOTS AND SMART COMPUTERS

The robots are coming. There's no question about *if,* only *when.* Look to the robot hobbyists for the shape of things to come. Whenever a tide of new technology washes over society, the hobbyists are the first to embrace that technology, shape it to personal needs, and give it a human form. This was the case with airplanes, spaceships, automobiles, and the radio. It is now true for computers and robots.

In cities and towns across America thousands of people are building their own robots. And it's not that difficult to do. You don't need a degree in electrical engineering or a small fortune to build a robot. Robot brains in the form of tiny computers are inexpensive and come prepackaged. Robot bodies can be built out of scrap metal, inexpensive, light plastics, and old motorcycle batteries. A working, computer-controlled robot might be built for under $200 today.

But another question altogether is, how smart are these robots going to be? At present, robots are mental dwarves. There are still real problems connected with robot voice-recognition, robot eyes, and a robot's ability to learn and solve problems. We live in a rapidly changing, extremely complex world. As yet there is no robot smart enough to be turned loose in it.

Nevertheless, robots (or computers) are getting smarter. Recently a computer program, BKG 9.8, beat the world backgammon champion and became the first computer program to defeat a world champion at any board or card game. And soon a computer will establish its superiority in other games—and in other areas—as well. Already computerized telephone operators are being tested. Their programs make them so smart and humanlike, it is often impossible to tell they are machines.

And look at the job robots are doing in factories. Texas Instruments has "seeing" blue-collar robots that work on the calculator assembly lines at a plant in Lubbock, Texas. Battelle Labs has a robot mouse that is so good getting through mazes, it may soon be running errands in underground mines. IBM has robots making new computers. And Matsushita Electric Company of Japan improved its production 2,900 percent when it replaced one hundred and twenty human employees with a computer, a robot team, and only four human monitors.

If robot and computer intelligence is improving so swiftly, how long will it be before they are more intelligent than people? And if that day comes, what is to prevent robots and computers from taking over management of people's lives and making all the decisions?

HERE COME THE ROBOTS

Just a few years ago, robots were the stuff of science fiction only, creatures of fantasy or the far-off future. Not so any longer. With the invention of the microcomputer, the tiny computer-on-a-chip, robots have come clattering from the future into the present. Already there are robot movie stars, blue-collar robots working in factories, robot kits, and homemade robots inventors put together in their basement workshop or on the kitchen floor.

Constructed out of modern lightweight plastics and metal alloys, the new robots employ the same microelectronic circuitry that has brought us digital watches, calculators, and school and home computers. By 1990, over ten million American families will have their own home computer. Shortly thereafter, just as many families will have a stable of robot

Battelle Laboratory's "Moonlight Special" maze-conquering robot mouse.

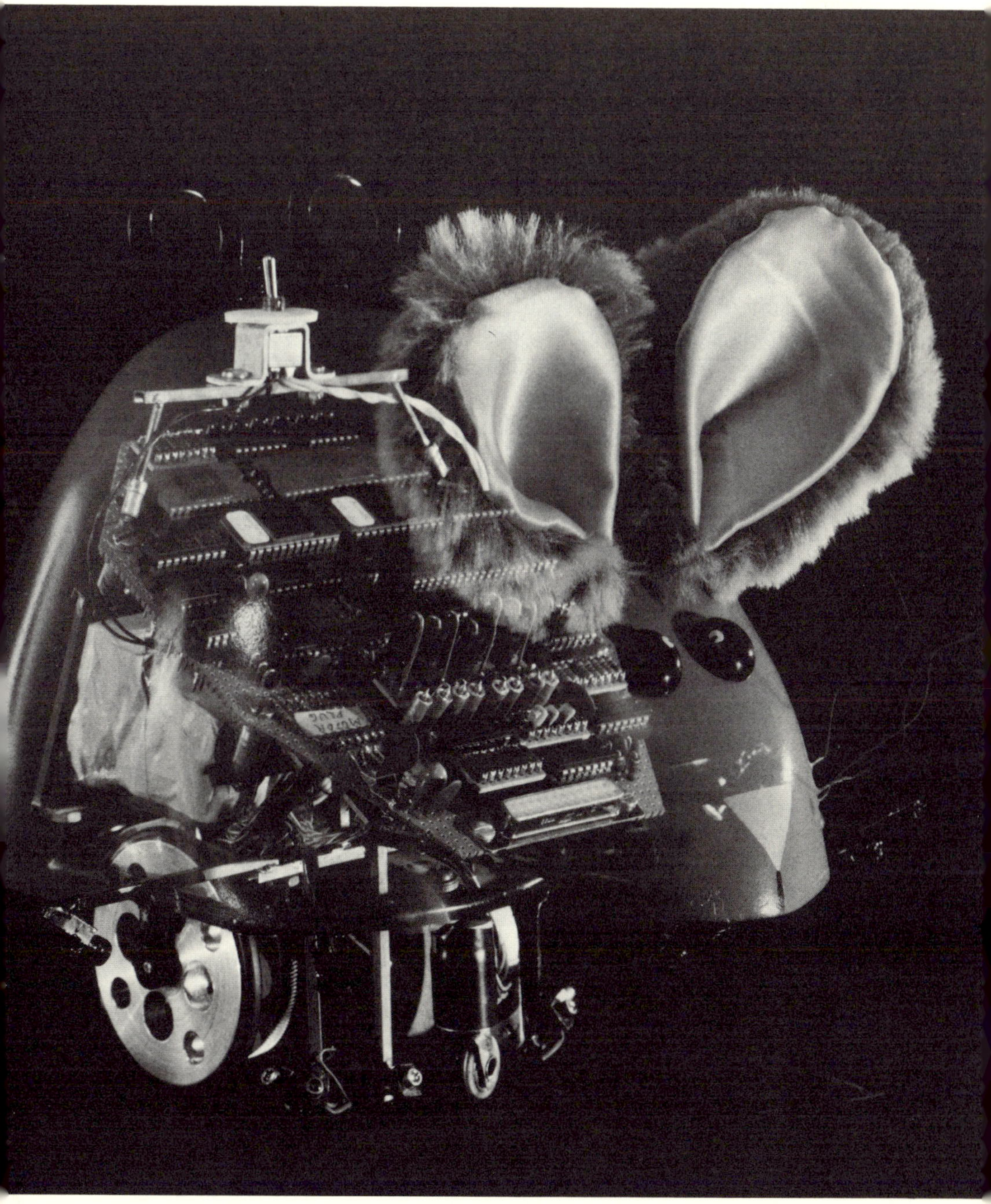

domestics programmed to tend to the sick or handicapped, clean the house and cook the meals, do yard work, babysit small children, and act as security guards. Family dogs and cats, move over! The robot, packaged as a cute little elf, a bumbling dragon, or a beefy butler, will soon become the family's new darling, its playmate and guardian.

Robots are already starting to turn up in people's homes. In the near future, expect one to move in near you—or come strolling through your front door. For example, there's Mike, a robot built by Tod Loofbourrow, a high school student in Westfield, New Jersey. Mike looks like a cross between a packing crate and a cash register, but he understands spoken commands such as "Go" and "Stop," and he "sees" by sending out high-pitched sound waves and then listening carefully for an echo, the way bats do.

Then there is Buster, built by David Heiserman of Columbus, Ohio. Buster, a pet robot, wanders from room to room until he gets "hungry." Then he searches for his battery recharger, rolls up to it, plugs himself in, and recharges.

There are also robot servants such as Arok, built by Chicago-area inventor Benjamin Skora. Arok vacuums the carpet, walks the dog, serves drinks, and answers the door. At 6 feet 8 inches (2 m), he is the ideal answer to pushy door-to-door salespeople.

Or take Elsie Toosee, a robot maid built by a couple in Kalamazoo, Michigan. Elsie resembles a trash can and makes weird noises, but she can carry groceries like an expert.

Some robots have brains, others feelings. Moonlight Special, built by Art Boland of Richland, Washington, and his friends, has special sensors and a microcomputer brain. Moonlight can travel down a 40-foot (12-m) maze, check

Tod Loofbourrow and Mike. Mike, for Microtron, can run at two different speeds and is strong enough to push or pull 150 pounds (67.5 kg) of weight.

out the deadends, and figure out the shortest path after only two tries. Another robot, Cosmo, broadcasts emotions on his TV-screen face. When Cosmo is angry, he frowns. When he is pleased, he smiles. And when he is annoyed, he screws up his face.

Finally, there are robot kits. For $400 you can build the ET-2 from Lour Control of Schaumburg, Illinois. ET-2 looks more like a three-layer cake than a robot, but it makes a reasonable pet. There's also the Grivet, a practical robot that comes equipped with arms. And then there's Unimate, an offspring of the new, intelligent robots used in manufacturing plants.

In the future, department stores will carry a full line of domestic robots. Your family might have a robot gardener to mow the lawn, trim the bushes, and weed the flowerbed. It might have a household-servant robot such as one being built by D. J. Reynolds of Lexington, Kentucky. Or it might have a crew of little robot mice to vacuum, wash, or wax the floor. If your family chooses mice helpers over a maid or butler, the mice will probably live in little "mouseholes" behind the baseboards in the walls. Once a week or so, your home computer will order them to "Clean up!" and they will scoot out of their holes, scurry around cleaning the house, then rush back to their holes.

There will also be personal robots, one for each member of your family. For example, your younger brother might have a robot buddy who will play with him, help him brush his teeth and take a bath, and read him bedtime stories. Your mom and dad will have robot bridge partners, a robot to help them when they bring work home from the office, and a robot cook to do the cooking and serve up dinner when they have to work late. And you'll have robots too, clever robots to play games with; hardy robots to play sports with; tutor robots to quiz you and help you with your homework; and comic robots who'll keep you laughing at their jokes and groaning at their terrible puns.

ROBOT INVENTORS

When Jonathan Kaplan was only eight or nine months old, he would lie alongside the washing machine and stare at the soapy, sudsy laundry tumbling and whirling about inside. This fascination for machines has never left Jonathan. Today, at seventeen, he is working on his ninth robot.

Jonathan's definition of a robot is "any machine with a stored program that can alter its external environment." Jonathan began building robots ten years ago after watching a cartoon show with robots in it. He built most of his robots in a small closet laboratory in his bedroom. His first robots were crude machines, barely more than mechanical marionettes controlled by cords and pulleys. Then, in 1974, Jonathan built his first stored-program (computerized) robot.

Jonathan's new robots are mobile and independent and able to respond to voice commands. When Jonathan calls out certain letters in a certain pitch, the Electronic Workman, one of Kaplan's later robots, can move forward and backward, left and right, raise and lower its arm, and open and close its claw—all based on programs Jonathan has written and stored in the robot's memory.

The young inventor's newest robots are even more intelligent and versatile. One of them can even arm wrestle. Jonathan can program the level of strength his wrestler-robot has. Privately, the robot has Jonathan licked. But whenever he and his robot have a public match, Jonathan comes out on top!

Jonathan Kaplan is now in college, where he is less involved in building robots and more involved in robot applications and in the field of robot and computer intelligence. He hopes that some of the work he is doing now will lead to robots of the future that will assist surgeons in the operating room and that will do manual labor under hazardous conditions such as in outer space or in a nuclear power plant.

Building the Unicorn One

A new film in the *Star Wars* epic is playing at a theatre in Monroe, a middle-sized town just outside of Charlotte, North Carolina. It is getting near show time, and a long line has formed in front of the theatre. The box office is not open yet, and the crowd is growing impatient.

Just then a towering conglomeration of metal and plastic comes rolling around the corner of the theatre. "It's a robot!" someone cries. The children cheer, break from the line, and crowd around the robot. "Who are you?" they ask. "Are you from *Star Wars*?"

The robot is friendly and obviously likes all the attention it is getting. "I'm not from *Star Wars*," it says wistfully, "though I wish I were. I'm just a local robot. I'm here to entertain you until the box office opens. Would you like to hear a song?"

"Sure!" shout the children.

The robot begins singing a medley of songs from Walt Disney movies. The robot's voice is deep, gruff, and slightly off-key. Meanwhile, the box office opens, and the line quickly dwindles, then disappears. As the people go inside, they bid good-bye to the robot, who continues to sing.

After everyone has gone into the theatre, the robot stops singing. Twenty feet away, in the parking lot, a man walks around the back end of a car. He's carrying a small metal box covered with buttons and dials, and on his head is a radio headset—earphones, an antenna, and a microphone. Behind the microphone is a big grin.

"Come on," the man says to the robot. "Let's be heading home." The man presses a button and turns a dial. The robot begins rolling down the sidewalk toward the man.

Who are these two, the man and the robot? The man is Jim Gupton, a professional photographer, free-lance writer, teacher, and inventor. The robot is KBPG6001, his latest invention. Jim made the robot in the small workshop inside his apartment. The robot is radio-controlled. When anyone talks to it, a microphone onboard the robot relays the sound to Jim's headset. When the robot talks or sings, that's Jim's voice radioed from his mike to speakers located just behind the robot's mouth.

Jim teaches an electronics class at the nearby Union County Career Center. During the last year, with his guidance, Jim's students built their own robot, Unicorn One, the

Unicorn One, built by electronics instructor Jim Gupton and his students.

predecessor to KBPG6001. The class built the robot for $349. The only tools used were a hacksaw, a file, and an electric drill.

The project for Jim and his class next year will be to make both Unicorn One and KBPG6001 computer-controlled. That way, the next time KBPG6001 goes to the movies, he won't need Jim to go with him. But he might just ask out Unicorn One.

Robot Maids and Butlers

For most of his life, D. J. Reynolds was a design engineer at Westinghouse Corporation in Lexington, Kentucky. Since he retired in 1968, his single overriding goal has been to build what he calls "a multipurpose, electromechanical household servant." Translated, that's a robot that can act as a family's maid, butler, and cook.

Reynolds has done as much thinking about household-servant robots as anyone. The robot he is now building embodies that thinking. When it is completed, the robot will be able to do a wide variety of household chores, including washing the family's dirty clothes, sorting and putting away clean clothes, vacuuming carpets, dusting furniture, mopping floors, making beds, preparing and cooking meals, and washing windows and walls.

What will the robot be like? It will be tall and have telescoping arms. Yet it will only have the strength of a 90-pound (31.5-kg) human. This is a safety feature to keep the robot from running around the house like the proverbial bull in a china shop—trampling hapless members of the family who happen to get in the robot's path or smashing furniture to smithereens.

The robot will run on wheels with tires made of a hard woven material such as steel wool. This will prevent the robot from picking up every throw rug in its path. It will also

A Household Helper robot, designed and built by D. J. Reynolds.

prevent the robot from climbing stairs—another safety feature. Imagine, for example, that you are going up the stairs to your bedroom. You hear a noise at the top of the steps, and you look up and see your 300-pound (135-kg) robot maid bouncing down the steps toward you. Unaware that it has changed from a domestic servant into a domestic tank, the maid is still clutching miscellaneous mops, dustpans, brooms, and a sloshing, half-filled bucket of bleach and water!

The family will be able to program the robot on a seven-day cycle but will also be able to make last-minute changes—such as a different dinner menu—as they are needed. A family that acquires a robot similar to Reynolds's servant might have to make adjustments in its daily routine. More important, the family as a whole would have to become more orderly so as not to interfere with the robot's work. This would include remembering to put the jelly back after you make a sandwich and not leaving homework, books, game boards, or furniture in any of the robot's frequently used paths (though the robot could maneuver itself around most of these obstacles).

Ideally, your household-servant robot will have a mechanical buddy to help it out of the tight fixes it is bound to get itself into. Both robots will probably be programmed from a home computer. This will allow them to be lighter and smarter, since they can take advantage of the stationary computer's superior memory and speed.

Finally, all sorts of special programming problems are sure to emerge once you put your household servant into action. For example, let's say your family decides, on the spur of the moment, to catch a quick movie before dinner one Friday night. The only problem is, you forget to tell the robot. At precisely 4:00 P.M., the robot receives orders from the household computer to start fixing dinner. It whips up a beautiful roast, baked potatoes, a salad, and cherry tarts for dessert. Dinner is served, steaming hot, at 6:00 P.M. At exactly 7:00 P.M., the robot gets the order to clean up. Oblivious to the fact that all the plates are still untouched and the dinner cold, it starts clearing the table. At 8:15 P.M. you arrive home, all hungry as bears—and find the house spic and span and your entire dinner in the garbage can!

IF YOUR TEACHER WERE A TURTLE

The Turtle is a robot produced by Terrapin, Inc., of Cambridge, Massachusetts. A Turtle resembles an electric can opener topped with a Kaiser-Bill helmet. Although it is cute, it is not very intelligent or independent—its orders come over a copper "umbilical cord" from a small computer. Yet the Turtle is versatile. Under control of the computer, it can emit beeps, flash lights, draw pictures with a pen screwed into its tummy, and wheel around a room strewn with obstacles such as tables, chairs, and people.

The Turtle can teach, too. Turtles are one of the highlights of an education project being conducted by the LOGO group at MIT in Cambridge, Massachusetts. The project, headed by Dr. Seymour Papert, has been in existence for over ten years and has developed a new approach to teaching young people that begins with real Turtles and continues with images of Turtles on a computer picture screen. The approach has had some real success in teaching art, mathematics, and the sciences, and in getting youngsters to take a more active role in their own education.

Dr. Papert's teaching method consists of beginning with some apparently trivial thought and gradually leading up to an extremely important or large idea or concept. The room where the Turtles roll about is known as Turtle World, one of many Microworlds Dr. Papert has created for students to learn in.

In the beginning students are taught in a real Microworld that has a real Turtle. Later on, the Microworld becomes a computer picture screen, and the Turtle, with its shapes and drawings, becomes an increasingly abstract image on the screen.

The only real rules in the Turtle World are the commands to the Turtle: FORWARD, BACK, RIGHT, LEFT, PENUP, PENDOWN, and so forth. After learning how to get the Turtle to put its drawing pen down (PENDOWN), the student can develop short, simple programs to make the Turtle draw geometric shapes and designs. One of the simplest yet most powerful programs a student can create is POLY to make the Turtle draw a polygon, or multisided two-dimensional figure.

Above: a Terrapin Turtle robot with geometric shapes drawn by the turtle on a screen, right. Using the LOGO language and the simple program POLY, a student can create even complex designs such as the one on the next two pages.

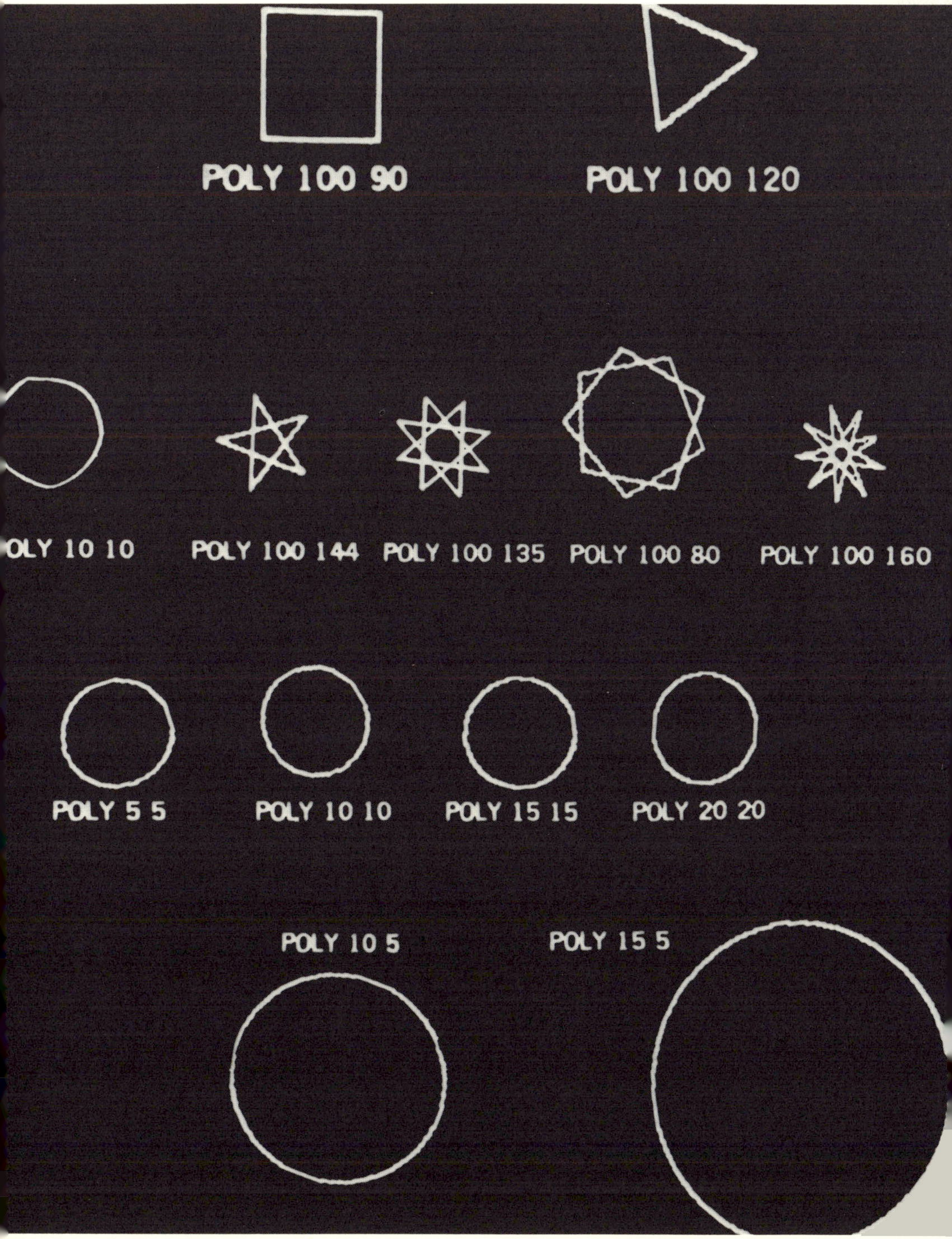
POLY 100 90
POLY 100 120
OLY 10 10
POLY 100 144
POLY 100 135
POLY 100 80
POLY 100 160
POLY 5 5
POLY 10 10
POLY 15 15
POLY 20 20
POLY 10 5
POLY 15 5

OLY 1000 110

In programming the Turtle to make various geometric shapes, students learn a great deal about programming, logic, and mathematics. Because in creating the program they must include instructions for the Turtle to stop and go and to move in different directions at different speeds, they also learn some concepts in physics, including Newton's first two laws of motion. Names such as "physics" make the concepts seem hard to understand, but watching the Turtle go through its motions brings those concepts down to earth.

At the end of a day spent in a Turtle World, the students leave feeling that the concepts learned that day, say from math and physics, are pretty obvious and "natural." The students may also have learned to play and experiment with those concepts by changing the Turtle's programs and inputs. Making the Turtle do new things and using it to explore new ideas are the most exciting aspects of Turtle learning.

CAN A COMPUTER THINK LIKE A PERSON?

How do small computers such as Texas Instruments' Speak & Spell and Boris, the chess-playing computer, work? By having programs—large, complex programs—stored in permanent memory. How do video computers such as Atari's Videogame and Mattel's Intellivision work? These computers have large programs, too. But their programs are stored in memory cartridges you plug into the computer.

Having the computer's program stored in permanent memory makes the computer fast, easy to operate, and automatically smart. But the programs are set and hidden inside a "black box." You can't write programs or make the programs already there better. And since you can't write programs, you miss the opportunity to teach the computer.

The way to make the computer learn is for you to write the learning program yourself—using, of course, a programmable computer. But be careful. The computer is a lot like a small, curious child asking questions. The child's intellectual development will depend a great deal on the type of answers it receives. The same goes for the computer.

But is it really possible to make a computer smart? That is, can a computer become as smart as you or me—or even smarter? And if it really has a "mind" of its own, can it suffer mental breakdowns, go insane, get angry, or grow depressed? And what about its moral values, its ethics? Will a smart computer be a good computer? Or might it become evil instead?

These are questions that scientists around the world are today trying to find answers to. In the end they really all boil down to a single question: Can a computer think like a person? So far, this question has gone unanswered. The difficulty is that thinking, or intelligence, can be looked at in many different ways. For example, does a computer's thinking have to exactly mimic the way people think? If so, things can get pretty complicated. There may be dozens of levels of human thinking and dozens of types. The conscious mind is certainly different from the subconscious mind. And what about dreams, imagination, instinct, and intuition? What about the various components of thinking, including the control and monitoring of bodily functions? What about the heart, the soul, shyness, fear, neurons, synapses, ganglia, biochemical reactions, and the like? To say the least, it is asking a lot to require a computer to think like a human being in order to be intelligent.

And anyhow, is a computer thinking if it can imitate what people do? If a computer can carry on a conversation, perform a simple task, learn something new, reason out a problem, beat a human at cards, or figure out how to cope with a strange situation, is it then intelligent?

Some scientists take a simulation, or modeling, approach to designing computers. They try to understand the way people actually think and then reproduce that process in the machine. Other scientists follow another route, called the engineering approach. It doesn't matter to these scientists whether or not computers imitate humans in terms of how they think, just so long as they can process data intelligently.

Artificial intelligence, the science that explores ways of increasing machine intelligence, is a controversial science. Human beings have been the smartest creatures on earth for millions of years. They aren't likely to give up that role without a fight. Sometimes, in order to demonstrate their innate superiority to machines, people point to humanity's greatest achievements—the music of Bach, Mozart, and Beethoven; the science of Galileo, Newton, and Einstein; the paintings of Raphael, Michelangelo, and Rembrandt. A computer could not achieve such heights of creativity, the critics say. Though convincing, this argument has a fallacy, namely that these were the most intelligent human beings in all of history. They were geniuses, but geniuses are rare. To be human you do not need the intelligence of a genius. The same goes for computers; they can be "intelligent" without having to be geniuses.

But how can a computer be intelligent at all? Doesn't a computer run on programs, programs made of commands you enter? There's a short rhyme to this effect:

Computers only do
What you tell them to.

This is true. But think of the case of a small child. Initially, the child knows few rules and has little experience. The child's parents can often predict what the child will do in a given situation. However, as the child has new experiences, learns new rules, and acquires new information, it becomes increasingly difficult to predict how the child will react to a familiar situation and even more difficult to guess how the child might react to a new situation.

The same is true for computers. With simple programs based on a few trivial commands, they are predictable. However, after their programs have been modified, after new data is thrown in, and after dozens of new programs have been added with hundreds or thousands of new commands, then their reactions to new situations—new data—become difficult to predict. Depending on the programs and the data, they have been known to act willful and independent, almost like a headstrong child.

A number of people see smart, thinking computers in the very near future. After all, they argue, with the new advances in technology, computers will soon be so fast and have such enormous memories, they will easily be as smart as people. Like the other arguments, this one, too, is convincing. But like the other arguments, it has a fallacy, since speed and memory, by themselves, are not enough to make a computer intelligent. Take the case of solving problems. Although every solvable problem has a list of solutions, only with trivial problems is the list a small one. Even average-sized problems, such as those we cope with daily, have huge or even infinite lists.

For example, take a problem such as how to win at chess. Being good at chess requires intelligence, yet chess is still just a game, and as a game it is far less complicated than real life. Nevertheless, chess is full of problems with solution lists that are immensely long. There are, for example, approximately 10-to-the-120th-power possible opening moves in chess! (This is 10 × 10 × 10 × 10 ×—ten multiplied by ten 120 times.) If speed and memory were all it took to be intelligent, we'd never have intelligent computers.

To further prove this point, let's say that archaeologists just dug up the ultimate computer. They trace its birth back billions of years, to the beginning of the universe. They discover it does all of its computing at the speed of light. And the number of bits of data its memory holds is equal to all of the atoms in the universe. Let's say also that archaeologists discover that this computer began searching for the best opening move in a game of chess on the day the universe was born. Has it found the answer yet? No. It is still churning away, trying to examine and evaluate all of the moves. After billions of years of speed-of-light searching and comparing, the machine still has a long way to go.

Today's scientists are aware of this pitfall and are attempting to create new computers that solve problems not by trying an exhaustive search of answers but by using *heuristic methods* such as insight, intuition, and experience. These methods are harder to describe and program, but they result in much faster problem-solving.

WHO'S SHARPER, US OR THEM?

One way to see if computers are intelligent is to use a modified *Turing Test,* invented by the great computer theorist Alan Turing. On one side of a wall is a computer and a person. On the other side is another person. The three communicate using typewriter keyboards and picture screens. The person who is alone can communicate with both the other person and the computer. However, he or she is not told which is which. The goal is to ask questions of both that will enable the questioner to tell the computer and the person apart. If the questioner is still stumped at the end of the session and cannot tell the computer from the person, the computer passes the test—it is intelligent.

Although no computer has yet passed a general Turing Test, where the questions can be on any subject, computers have done surprisingly well in special categories. For example, people have not been able to tell the computer and the person apart when the questions are on chess, bridge, and—of all things—mental health!

Some of the smartest computers today are robots, including the homemade robots built by young inventors such as Tod Loofbourrow. Other smart robots are the chess-playing robots and laboratory robots such as Shakey and WABOT-1. Even so, although these robots are good at certain tasks, they still lack a generalized intelligence that would qualify as human.

For example, the chess-playing computers can defeat highly ranked amateur human chess players. To do this, they must be intelligent. But that's all they can do. By human standards, if a person were a whiz at chess but could do nothing else, it is unlikely he or she would get high marks for brains. And that brings us back to our original question. If a computer beats us at some game or task, who is smarter—it or us? Our answer—for now anyway—is probably that we are.

Today's computers, then, are not really as smart as people. But how about the small computers of the future? Remember, research into artificial intelligence has been going on for a mere twenty years. People have been around for millions of years. In a very short time, the distance between human and computer intelligence has narrowed dramatically. According to Alan Turing, although we now question whether machines can think, before the end of this century the answer will be so obvious that we will have given up the debate.

SMALL COMPUTERS, THE FUTURE, AND YOU

Imagine waking up starving one night in the future. You just bailed out of a nightmare in which you were a prisoner-of-war and were slowly dying from a lack of food and malnutrition. You'd love a drumstick from that leftover turkey in the refrigerator, but you're really too tired and more than a little frightened thanks to the dream. All in all, you'd rather not get out of bed.

Is there any way to get that turkey leg? Yes. You can have Muffin, your robot monkey, bring it to you. Do you need to call out to Muffin and risk waking up your parents? No. Thanks to the new telepathic computers, you can summon your pet with nothing more than amplified brain waves.

You lie back in bed, close your eyes, and think a succession of telepathic commands: MUFFIN . . . FRIG . . . MEAT . . . BOTTOM SHELF . . . BRING HERE . . . NOW.

Finished with your message, you burrow deep into your pillow and begin to doze off. All of a sudden you are awakened. Something is nudging you. It's Muffin sticking you in the ribs with the turkey leg.

Recent developments in brain-wave research and in computer-brain interaction indicate that some telepathic communication between brains and computers may one day be possible. And there are other possible developments as well, most of them more imminent, such as a computer-controlled house and an electronic telephone booth with giant picture screens on all four walls. One day you may find yourself inside such a booth carrying on a five-way computer-monitored conversation with friends and relatives from all over the country.

THE MIND READER

Human brains and electronic brains are vastly different in the way they process information. Small computers have electronic brains that are made of crystalline semiconductors such as rubies and silicon. The crystals in the semiconductors are arranged in an array, or lattice. The computer's brain carries information in the form of electrons flowing through the lattice. Humans, on the other hand, have organic brains made of colloids, spongy materials with suspended atoms and large molecules. The human brain carries information using large molecules and charged atoms.

The human brain is more complex than the computer brain, but the computer brain is much faster. For example, the fastest nerve cells in your body carry electrical impulses at a rate of 65½ feet (20 m) a second. A computer brain can operate a billion times faster. Yet your brain makes up for its relative slowness by being able to process large numbers of commands at the same time, while the computer brain can handle only one command at a time. The human brain does this by *multiplexing,* or splitting up nerve impulses, sending them in many directions at once, then regrouping them after they have been processed. Thus, although a computer can solve a math problem in a millionth of a second, in precisely the same instant your brain is monitoring and controlling your internal organs, your nervous system, your muscular system, and so on. It is receiving and processing sensory input from your eyes, nose, tongue, skin, ears, and elsewhere. It is also thinking, dreaming, speculating, planning, and feeding you lines so you have something to say.

Yet as different as they are, human and computer brains also have some important things in common. For example, they both use electrical impulses organized into a binary code (ones and zeros) to store and transmit information. Computers switch circuits on and off; people have neurons that either fire electrical impulses or do not. Because of these shared characteristics, it seems likely that sometime in the future it will become possible to link human and computer brains. For what purpose? To create a new version of Frankenstein's monster? Nothing as dramatic—or gruesome—as this. A more realistic and constructive purpose would be to have the computer brain act as an intelligence amplifier for the human brain. The human-machine, or *bionic,* brain would be a powerful combination of the computer brain's speed and the human brain's ability to multiplex, or do several things at the same time. When will we have the technology to build this bionic brain? It's too soon to tell. But one thing is certain. A bionic brain will not just affect a person's intelligence. It will also have a profound impact on his or her emotions, actions, self-image, and perceptions of the environment.

Is it just fantasy to think of linking a human brain with a computer? Not at all. Already, researchers in the Defense Department's Advanced Research Projects Agency have been able to translate some of the human brain's electrical impulses—in the form of electroencephalograms (EEGs)—into specific thoughts and signals to different parts of the body. Elsewhere, at New York University, scientists have constructed a device that picks up magnetoencephalograms (MEGs) from the brain. A MEG is far more sensitive than an EEG to specific brain messages and commands.

If present experiments continue, it won't be long before scientists construct a device that can relay a human brain's MEG to a computer. Once this becomes possible, you will be able to think up a command to a computer and send it directly to the computer's brain. You won't type anything on a keyboard. You won't say anything. You'll think your command, and the computer will read your mind.

THE TOOTH-FILLING COMPUTER

In the not-so-distant future, it's possible that people won't have to lug their new computer through the front door. Instead, they'll carry it inside their body—in their brain to control tremors, amnesia, or epilepsy; in their chest to regulate heartbeats; even in their tooth fillings, to act as miniature calendars, calculators, or clocks. Who knows, if computers become small enough, smart enough, and learn to read your mind, a tooth-filling computer might be just the thing. It wouldn't need to talk. It would communicate with you by sending "telepathic" brain messages. It might communicate in English or in pure concepts, ideas, or sensations.

The computer could have a wealth of information stored inside it, including an encyclopedia, a dictionary, the morning newspaper, joke books, sports and movie trivia, and so forth. It could help you with your schoolwork, give you advice, recite poetry, and play music. Like Jiminy Cricket in Walt Disney's *Pinocchio,* it might even turn out to be a second conscience!

THE INVISIBLE COMPUTER

What does a computer look like? Many people see the computer as a huge metal box with blinking lights, miles of wires, spinning tape drives, and computer punch cards with little square holes.

Some computers of today look like this, but not small computers. A small computer isn't big at all; in fact, it fits on a desk or table. It has a picture screen, typewriter keys, a box containing the circuit boards, and perhaps some add-ons such as a printer, a microphone, some game paddles, a speaker, a place to plug in memory cartridges, or a tape recorder or disk drive.

This image of a small computer might be very familiar to you. But don't get used to it. Small computers are changing rapidly.

Ten years from now, you won't have one or two small computers in your classroom or home, you'll have dozens. But they won't be sitting out for you to see them. They'll be built into your school desk or the wall or hidden in a cupboard or under a counter. They'll be permanent fixtures that come with the school building or home. When a real estate broker tries to sell your family a new house, he or she will be sure to mention the computer:

> This is a lovely little home, folks. And the best feature is the computer, the fast, polite Super Butler 2001. This little computer, located in the kitchen between the microwave oven and the trash recycler, is a great labor saver. It controls all of the house's appliance computers along with a fleet of

household robots that take care of all the messy little chores around the house. You won't have to lift a finger.

The Super Butler's printers are built into tables, desks, the TV, and the kitchen countertop. When one is ready to print, a little door slides back, and the paper spews out. But there won't be much paper, since there is a picture screen on almost every wall, and most of the items you print will be on erasable microfilm that can be recycled and fed back into the computer.

There is also no need for tape recorders, floppy disk drives, or memory packs. The Super Butler's mass-storage memory is located in bubble devices behind the walls. When you need a new game or learning program, you just order it out loud over the phone, the cable TV, or the household intercom. All are linked to the computer. The Butler will place your order with a store's computer that will send the game, then call the bank computer to have it transfer the cost of the game from your checking account to the store's account.

As you know, there are special-purpose computers inside almost every device in the home. The old-fashioned electrical outlets in the house have all been replaced with E & I (electricity and information) outlets.

Every outlet is a connection with the Super Butler computer, so wherever you find an outlet, you can plug in game paddles, light pens, your Dynabook for recharging or reprogramming, and so forth.

Computer microphones and speakers are built into walls all around the house. You won't see the Super Butler. Yet it will be all around you, looking after you, doing errands for you, waiting to serve you.

Having this invisible computer will be like owning a magic lamp with a genie inside to grant you your every wish. "Your wish is my command," the genie used to say. That's what Super Butler says, too.

THE INTELLIGENT HOUSE

The small computer of the future will be like the Super Butler computer in the previous chapter. It will have the speed, processing power, and memory to tie into almost every appliance in your home. It is likely that when homes are built in the future, they will have wall information outlets that connect the computer to the various appliances.

And after the Super Butler computer, what next? The next step is the Intelligent House. The small computer will be the house's "brain." Its "nervous system" will be all the electrical appliances—the telephone, the TV, the stereo, the washing machine, the drier, the air conditioner, the clocks, the house lights, the furnace, and so on. Like the computer "watchdogs" that people are already installing in their homes, the computer of the future will have sensors located everywhere. These will be its eyes and ears. With its electrical and mechanical appendages, a home computer will literally be tuned into most of what happens around your house, both inside and out.

Will it wait for you to give it orders? Not for most of its activities. If a section of the lawn becomes too dry, it will water it. If a room gets too warm, it will turn on the air conditioner. If another room gets too moist, it will turn on the dehumidifier. It will wake you in the morning with a cheery "Hello" and play your favorite music to lull you to sleep at night. It will warn you in case of emergency, answer the phone when you're not home, and call the doctor in case of an accident. It will have a personality, too. It'll do so many things and be so much a part of your life, you may begin to regard it as a member of your family.

There is an excellent short story by Ray Bradbury about an intelligent house. The title of the story is "There Will Come Soft Rains." Bradbury wrote the story thirty years ago, but he was able to anticipate the coming of the computers that will make a house such as this possible.

ELECTRONIC MAIL

In Great Britain it's called Ceefax and Prestel; in France it's Antiope; in the United States it's called Teletext. What is it?

It's the transmission of information—in the form of words and colorful pictures—by your local TV station. If your TV has a "decoder," it will be able to pick up the words and pictures and display them in page form on your TV, just as you would display them on a small computer.

TV stations send radio signals through the air. Your TV antenna picks up these signals. Once inside the TV, they are amplified and separated into sound and picture signals that are sent to the TV's speakers and its picture tube. Guided by the signals, an electron gun inside the TV creates images on the screen by firing streams of electrons that fill the entire screen thirty times a second—just fast enough to fool the human eye into seeing one continuous moving picture.

In order to draw an accurate picture, the electron gun has to retrace some of its movements. During the fraction of a second it is doing this, a *piggyback signal* can be sent by the TV station. This is the Teletext signal. With a special decoder installed on the TV and with a hand-held keyboard, you can replace the regular TV program on your screen with the Teletext picture page.

The Viewdata system is somewhat different. With Viewdata, the teletext signal is sent over the phone line from a central Viewdata computer. Using an *acoustic coupler* or a *modem* attached to the telephone, your TV can be linked to the computer. The British Post Office, Viewdata's sponsor, has provided over 200,000 pages of information for Viewdata subscribers, including an entire 60,000-page encyclopedia. And if you want to save information, there's a special hookup that allows you to plug a tape recorder into the telephone.

New products are already appearing that anticipate the widespread use of Teletext. For example, Matsushita Electric of Osaka, Japan, recently introduced Picture Paper, a TV containing a multicolor printing press that enables you to make a color copy of the text and pictures sent over your TV.

Another way to transmit information is over the radio. Recently Jim Warren, president of Digital Wireless, Inc., began what he calls the Datacast Project. If the project is a success, in the near future a wide variety of computerized messages and pictures will be broadcast over FM radio stations.

The next step is to tie your small computer into Teletext or Datacast. This is already being done in the case of cable TV. In the United States, commercial TV stations are broadcasting Teletext, and cable TV stations are broadcasting Cabletext. For example, Six Star Cablevision in Los Angeles has begun marketing a system linked to a Mattel Intellivision computer that they will install for you in your home. Six Star broadcasts over fifty different computer programs along with its normal TV broadcasts.

Eventually you will keep your small computer plugged in to TV and radio broadcasts twenty-four hours a day. It will have a program inside it that will constantly check for information you are especially interested in, including events such as concerts and sales, weather reports, sports information, school closings, record store and movie ads, and local news. Whenever it sees something it will store a copy on bubble memory and also print out a note to you on the printer in the kitchen or at your desk. It might even create an electronic newspaper for you each day that contains information the computer thinks you would like to see.

You could also use the small computer along with Teletext for buying and selling things. For example, if you were interested in selling an old camera or a pair of skis, you would just type an ad into the computer. It would send the ad to the classified ad list circulating via Teletext throughout the community. If someone wanted the skis or the camera, his or her computer would receive a message and either prepare a note for the family bulletin board or flash a red light at the keyboard, indicating that it had some important news.

One of the best ways to use a combined small computer and Teletext system would be to send electronic mail. You could type your letters to friends and relatives on the computer keyboard, and the computer would "mail" them by sending them over the cable or phone line to their destination. Regular mail sometimes takes several days or longer to go from one place to the next. Your electronic letters would only take a few minutes—possibly only a few seconds.* Also, since pictures, voices, music, and even game-

---

* The new phone rates for electronic mail will probably start with the "first three seconds" rather than the customary voice-call rate of "the first three minutes."

boards can all be digitized, your electronic letter need not be limited to only letters and words.

Computers and Teletext systems will benefit everyone, but think what they'll mean to the home-bound—invalids, handicapped people—people who cannot leave their homes for one reason or another. Without even getting up from a couch, a bed, or a wheelchair, a person will be able to shop for groceries, buy medicine, send and receive letters, read electronic copies of books and magazines from the library, even vote. The small computer linked to Datacast on the radio and Teletext on TV will help these people especially lead more active and meaningful lives.

THE END OF SCHOOL?

In the next few years, small computers will appear in many people's homes and will play a large part in family entertainment and education. Since these computers will be great teachers, will that mean the end of school?

No. But why not? Because as powerful an educational tool as the computer is going to be, it cannot take the place of a good teacher or a roomful of classmates. Using a small computer on your own, you'll learn rapidly. But combine the graphics and modeling ability of a small computer with the guidance and encouragement you can get from your teacher, and the enthusiasm and debate you're sure to get from your classmates, and you have an unbeatable learning combination—one no machine on its own can duplicate.

Besides, there are many other advantages in going to school. There are school athletics, clubs, the student council, the chorus, art and drama classes, and the band. There's all the science and laboratory equipment and all the art supplies that you'd never be able to afford at home. And there are parties, dances, and get-togethers with friends who can teach you things that would make a computer "tilt."

On the other hand, the computer is going to have a huge impact on schooling. For example, every classroom will soon have its own small computer. Your teachers will no longer need to stand up and teach four, five, six, or seven hours a day. They'll record their lessons on videodisks and let the computer take over much of the repetitious work and drilling that are necessary parts of learning.

Many schools today are in financial trouble. Once there is a small computer in almost every person's home, however, schools can declare several "home days" each term, in order to save money. A home day will be a day you don't have to report to school, but it won't be a vacation day either. You'll have plenty of schoolwork—most of it to be done on your home computer.

On a home day, when you have finished a lesson, your homework, or even a test, your home computer will automatically dial up the school's computer and send your work in for the computer to grade and for your teacher to review. Within an hour or two, your computer will be blinking its red lights or announcing over the intercom that it has gotten your work back. The work will be graded, probably have a few comments from your teacher, and be followed by a new assignment. You'll be kept so busy on a home day, you'll probably be looking forward to the next regular school day, when you can take it a little easier!

THE ENCHANTED COMPUTER

Computer: *You've just entered the Troll Room, a tiny cramped hole with passages to the east and south and a forbidding cave leading west. The walls are marred by ugly gouges and rusty splashes of caked, dried blood.*

Ahead of you stands a nasty-looking Troll, brandishing a razor-sharp ax and blocking all passages out of the room. Your sword begins to glow brightly.

You: *WOUND TROLL WITH SWORD*

Computer: *Your blow lands but bounces harmlessly off the Troll's armored shoulder. The Troll swings his ax, and it nicks your arm as you dodge.*

You: *AGAIN*

Computer:	*The quickness of your thrust stuns the Troll and knocks him back. The Troll slowly regains his feet.*
You:	*AGAIN*
Computer:	*A quick stroke, but the Troll is on guard. He sidesteps, and your sword misses. He swings his ax, aiming for your head.*
You:	*DUCK*
Computer:	*The ax grazes your head, lopping off a few hairs, then crashes into a stalactite, producing a shower of blue and white sparks that leaves you momentarily blinded.*
You:	*WOUND TROLL WITH SWORD*
Computer:	*You miss the Troll but catch your sword on his scabbard strap. The Troll loses his footing and falls. You leap over him. This is your chance to escape!*

Quick! Which passage do you choose? Should you try the passages leading east and south or the "forbidding" cave leading west?

Are you caught up in the action? If you are, you're not alone. So are millions of other people all around the world. They're all playing "epic fantasy games" (also called "fantasy role-playing games"), using either a computer or a human Game Master.

The scene above is a variation of a scene found in *Zork: The Great Underground Empire,* one of the most popular "CFSGs" (computer fantasy and simulation games). In *Zork* and in another, equally popular, game called *Adventure,* the computer plays the part of the Game Master. It acts as your eyes and ears and guides you through the treacherous fantasy world. It sets up terrifying situations, then waits for you to tell it what you plan to do. Depending upon the situation, you might need to fight, run, hide, find a clue, use one of your "possessions," or remember a magic word. It's up to you to figure out which. Make the right choice, and you might come away with a fabulous treasure. Make the wrong choice, and you'll be lucky to escape alive.

What makes epic fantasy games so popular? First and

foremost, it is because *you* are the central character, the hero or heroine. Second, the games are challenging. Some take hours or even days to play to conclusion. Third, the games are surprising and unpredictable. Around the next bend may lie a fierce, hungry dragon, a golden chalice full of sapphires and diamonds, a bottomless pit, or nothing at all. You never know which. Fourth, winning a game depends on any number of factors, including skill, courage, wisdom, wit, strength, sorcery, or just plain luck. Often as you get better at it, the game automatically grows more difficult. Fifth, fantasy games have an infinite number of possible endings. If you're playing a game, and a trail, a cave, or a castle looks familiar, don't count on it. As soon as your guard is down, that's when a howling dwarf leaps on your shoulders, a trap door flies open, or a barrage of poison-tipped darts fly at you from a darkened corridor.

CFSGs in the Future

CFSGs of the present are absorbing, exciting, and are played by tens of thousands of enthusiasts. But they can't even begin to compare—either in concept or execution—with the games that will appear over the next decade. According to Dennis Allison, a game expert: "Most games are built around the simple 'explore and collect' scenario. Interaction with the fantasy environment is limited by the computer hardware on the one hand and by the limitations of the software on the other." Most of the games consist of a written (textual) dialogue between the game player and the computer. They are "solitaire" and therefore permit only one player. Graphics are limited to simple lists, tables, maps, and two-dimensional cartoon or stick figures. Music and sound effects are still primitive. Game scenarios, though complicated and absorbing, are still rudimentary, repetitive, and superficial. And the senses of touch, taste, and smell are never brought into play.

But all this is changing. New computer technologies will soon be available. New software will soon be developed based on findings in artificial intelligence. And there is a growing realization of the wide range of dramatic plots suitable for CFSGs. Soon CFSGs won't be limited to sword-

and-sorcery, science fiction, and horror plots. There will also be historical romance CFSGs, mystery CFSGs, even biography CFSGs in which the player conducts a simulated interview with anyone in history—from Cleopatra to Adolf Hitler.

As humans, our most used senses are our eyes and ears. Our preferred way to communicate is by talking and listening. In the near future, CFSGs will become less textual ("word-oriented," or booklike) and more audiovisual. The most important technology spurring this transition will be the videodisk. A standard disk will soon be available for less than $10 and will carry an hour or more of pictures and sounds that can be used as part of a computerized epic fantasy game.

And what about smell, taste, and touch? In the 1950s someone proposed that TV include "smell-o-vision," where odors could be created and tied to the action on television. It's not hard to imagine CFSGs with chemically synthesized odors wafted by a small fan over the picture screen and controlled by the computer. Also, one can imagine headgear with a little nozzle aimed at your mouth. With a cue from the computer, the nozzle would squirt different chemicals into your mouth to give you a "taste" of the action occurring in the game. Finally, a CFSG could have "feelies" in the form of electrodes attached to your brain or devices installed in your easy chair. The devices would give you a feeling of being transported into the game world inside the computer.

Telepresence

Marvin Minsky, an expert in robotics and artificial intelligence at MIT in Cambridge, Massachusetts, predicts that, with sufficient research and development, we will be able to construct smart, sensor-laden robots that will work, say, on the ocean floor or in a lunar quarry while their human operators—wearing wired-up bodysuits—are safe and cozy in their own homes. Minsky calls these robots *telepresences,* and he feels that the special bodysuits will be so constructed as to give the remote human operator such a barrage of sensory information from the robot that the operator will feel as if he or she *is* the robot doing the robot's work. The person will "see" through the robot's eyes, hear what the robot hears, feel the heat, the cold, the vibrations, the pressures, and the textures the robot feels. When the person raises an arm, the robot will raise its arm. When the person positions the robot's hand to grab a tool, as the robot's hand closes around the tool, the operator will feel the tool in his or her own, gloved hand, will feel the tool's weight, its mass, its contours, and its textures, even though the operator's own hand is empty. Although the human operator will not be present at the bottom of the ocean or on the surface of the moon, he or she will, in the form of a robot, be *telepresent.*

Similarly, ultrasophisticated CFSGs will eventually be constructed in which the game players achieve the same or even superior telepresence in the game's environment as the human operator does through his or her robot extension. Imagine getting ready for a fantasy game by putting on a costume that resembles an astronaut's spacesuit. The facemask on the suit would be opaque since it was, in fact, a miniature three-dimensional holographic picture screen.

Next you would enter a totally empty padded room. When you were ready to make your "voyage" or "journey" to the computer's fantasy world, you would simply say something like, "ALIEN WILDERNESS PLANET—BEGIN." A fraction of a second later—according to all your senses—you would actually be on the game planet. You would see, feel, taste, smell, and hear everything from the perspective of a being on that planet. If you had chosen a being who was 20 feet (6 m) tall, you would see everything from 20 feet (6 m) above the ground. Also, if you were playing a group game with your friends, you would see them, too, in the roles they had chosen to play.*

---

* The telepresence version of the CSFGs was foreshadowed by Arthur C. Clarke in his stories *Against the Fall of Night* and *The City and the Stars.*

COMPUTER MOVIES

Many of today's big corporations use a computer system called SynthaVision to create the dazzling ads you see on television. Small computers of the future will allow you, in your home, to use systems such as SynthaVision to produce colorful, animated computer "movies."

How would you use SynthaVision? Let's say you wanted to produce a three-dimensional picture of a complex geometric object such as the dish on a radio telescope. First, you would type in a short description of the dish, then you would type in "MOVEMENT" and "COLOR" commands. The computer would do the rest. It would draw the object, display it, and allow you to rotate it in any direction, just as if it were real.

Sophisticated computer animation systems are used to produce many of the special effects you see in today's science fiction and adventure movies. During a live-action filming, for example, movie technicians can project a human actor onto a scene created by a computer. The scene is called a *matte.*

At one time, all mattes were painted by artists. Whenever an especially complex, elegant, or out-of-the-ordinary scene was called for in a movie script, a matte would be painted, because the scene would be too time-consuming or too expensive to actually stage.

Even today, some mattes are still stationary paintings. Sections of mattes are blacked out so that when the film showing the matte and the film showing the actors are merged, the result is realistic-looking. Some of the best mattes ever created were painted by the artist Peter Ellenshaw for the Walt Disney movies *Mary Poppins* and *The Black Hole.*

Now, computers can produce mattes, but mattes that move and have a life of their own. Computers can also project the actors onto the living, moving matte. The scene can be a representation of anything or anyplace in the universe. Or its design can come from the imagination.

Computers that today make animated movies, mattes, and commercials are very expensive, even for commercial use. Fortunately, though, less expensive systems are on the way.

Small computers of the future will produce high-quality animated images that you can control and change. Any three-dimensional image you can dream up will be possible to produce. And it won't stand still. It will move at your command. Even more exciting, by using a video camera (and a videotape or videodisk recorder), you will be able to take pictures of real people and mix them with scenes you've created on the computer.

This will make for some stunning computer home movies. For a space war movie you might program the computer to create mattes of suns going nova, comets hitting planets, or gaping black holes swallowing galaxies. Or, using your videodisk recorder, you could film shots of yourself in your own living room taking part in a great battle scene.

And that's still not all. You will also be able to program the computer to play music during the movie and to add special sound effects. The computer will mix the sound effects, the matte, and the pictures you have taken, and come up with a movie.

The universe may be a big place, but your imagination is even bigger. How about scenes from other universes? Think of the epic fantasy games you could create, the detective movies, the adventure or suspense films. You could program the computer to paint mattes of your favorite scenes from the comics, mystery thrillers, horse stories, or science fiction novels.

Once you are done making your computer movie, you will be able to show it on a large-screen TV. Three-dimensional images will leap from the screen into your living room. Already in the Soviet Union and in some laboratories in the United States, scientists are filming three-dimensional movies using laser cameras and a technique known as *holography*. When this technique is perfected and becomes available on small computers, you will be able to make all your movies or games in three dimensions. By projecting them in 3-D, the real and fantastic images you create will become more dramatic and more alive than ever.

Let's say it's the year 1995, and you want to play an epic fantasy game using a small computer that's equipped with all the gadgets for making computer movies. To get started, you turn to a microphone embedded in the wall and say:

COMPUTER . . . DRAGON MAZE . . . ALL PROPS . . . EXPERT

You've hardly finished issuing the commands when the room begins to darken. A huge labyrinth flashes on all four walls. A dragon's roar reaches your ears. You feel the dragon's scorching breath and smell its stench. You quickly plug the game controls into the nearest outlet, then clutch them tightly in both hands. The dragon rounds the corner of the maze and hurls itself into your living room. But you're already gone, racing along the corridors of the maze, searching for a way to escape. The dragon scrambles off the living room floor, then chases after you in hot pursuit.

THE DARKER SIDE OF WHAT THE FUTURE MIGHT BRING

Small computers of the future will be useful, educational, and entertaining. But there is another side, a darker side. In a technology as pervasive and powerful as small computers, there are sure to be abuses. Is government regulation the way to avoid those abuses? Or will intervention by the government lead to a form of "Big Brother," perhaps the worst abuse of all? And is "Big Brother" a technical possibility? These are some of the issues we will explore in this survey of the darker aspects of computer technology of the future.

THE TERRIBLE NEW WEAPONS

A small computer of the future will have the ability to send, receive, manipulate, and store huge quantities of information in only a fraction of a second. The computer will prepare an instant summary of all this information and give its owner the summary by means of voice or a visual display on its picture screen. For the computer owner the summary will represent new knowledge and thus greater power over his or her world.

Power on its own is neither good nor bad. It depends on how the power is used. We have seen some of the ways in which the power stemming from small computers can be put to good uses. Unfortunately, this new power can also be used for harmful or unlawful purposes—in warfare, espionage, terrorism, or crime.

Over the years the military has been one of the chief financial supporters of computer miniaturization. It is only natural that it would become one of the chief users of the new, smaller computers. It is almost an understatement to say that the future of warfare will be revolutionized by the addition of small computers to almost every type of weapon imaginable. There will be computerized rifles, cannons, tanks, missiles, torpedoes, bullets, and bombs. Every soldier in combat will carry a small computer to help keep in touch with the unit, locate the "enemy," and aim the rifle or other weapon in the enemy's direction.

Already small computers are appearing in a number of areas. For example the M60 army tank has a laser onboard that pinpoints a target. Then a small, specially designed computer aims the tank's guns and missiles.

The air force, too, makes extensive use of small computers. One plane, for example, is able to fly at high speeds only a few feet above the ground. In this way it avoids being detected by enemy radar. Of course no human would have quick enough reflexes to avoid all the trees, buildings, and other obstacles in the plane's path. The plane's pilot and navigator aren't human, though. They are a high-speed, "intelligent" computer.

Newer missiles, too, come with small computers, located, along with video cameras, in the missile's nose. Hughes Aircraft Company, for example, has developed new "seeing" missiles that can track moving targets on the ground—humans, tanks, supply trucks, and so on. The missile can "chase after" its target on its own, or it can relay pictures back to human operators, who give the missile new instructions.

Computer Crooks

Some smart, technologically sophisticated criminals are already misusing small computers in a number of ways. Many of the crimes being committed via computer are relatively petty. A favorite target is the phone system. For example some people have discovered ways their computer can tie into the phone system and "trick" it into letting them make an unlimited number of long distance calls free of charge. Other people have used computers to dial up hundreds of phone numbers—all within only a few seconds.

When someone picks up the phone, the computer plays a harassing "crank" message, then automatically hangs up.

Other criminal uses for computers are more serious and amount to felonies. For example already there are documented cases of small computers dialing up big bank and insurance company computers, "cracking" their security systems, and then ordering the computer to make deposits into an account that the criminal has taken out under a fictitious name. The criminal withdraws all the money from the account, then leaves town before anyone suspects anything.

In the 1960s and 1970s world leaders worried that terrorists would get ahold of nuclear bombs and use them to blow up their enemies or back up their demands. Today this worry is still present. But now there is a new worry—that terrorists will use small, powerful computers to commit acts of terrorism or extortion.

Who is most vulnerable to these acts? Some nations, including the United States, Japan, and parts of Western Europe, are highly computerized. Most of these nations depend on computers for their economic health and military preparedness. The "lifeline" of any huge computer network—and also its weak link—is the telephone. It is not hard to picture terrorists of the future using their own network of small computers to scramble and detour messages being sent over military or economic networks. And at present, there would be no easy way to track down terrorists and stop their damaging computer transmissions. Recovery from "electronic blackmail" might take months and cost billions of dollars. Government files and company records might be permanently destroyed; the programs that "drive" the computers and give them their orders might be sabotaged or erased. A country's computer networks could end up in a shambles as a result of computer terrorism.

THE INFORMATION BURGLAR

How does information percolate through society? Originally, it was by word of mouth. People went from place to place, met other people, and talked about what they had seen and what they knew. Later, other devices were used—couriers, messengers, pony express, a postal system. In most of these cases, the information was passed along as words on paper.

Today this is all changing. Newer systems of communication, including the telephone, radio, laser, microwave, and satellite systems, are replacing the old systems. Information passing through these systems is no longer represented as words on paper. Instead it is in the form of electronic pulses, radio waves, or sparks of amplified light. And now, with the introduction of computers, the rate of information flow has been stepped up dramatically. A fast pony—or even a fast plane—can no longer compete. Information is generated at a rate of thousands of bits a second, then thrown across states, countries, even continents, at the speed of light.

When most of society's information was on paper, it could be protected by fastened doors, padlocked bags, armed guards, or trusted couriers. But how do you guard beams of light or electronic pulses that appear, then vanish in a few millionths of a second? Data security—protection of information—is fast becoming one of society's most difficult and important problems.

Much of the information transmitted over the new systems of communication is sensitive, proprietary, or private. It belongs in the hands of its owner or with its owner's agent, friend, or client. It must not become easily available to third parties, including hostile countries, rival companies, or even casual observers.

Until recently, most computerized communications were sent or received by government agencies and large corporations. The arrival of the home computer—in the form of an electronic family record-keeping system—will change this. Home computers will soon store your family's most intimate and private information—its tax records, checking and savings account information, real estate records, financial records, medical records, even the family's private correspondence and diaries.

Having all of this information on a computer would not be a problem if the computer were isolated from the rest of the world. However, using the phone the computer can and must keep in touch with other computers—computers belonging to banks, government agencies, credit bureaus, department stores, employers, and friends and relatives, for example.

Literally speaking, the computer will be always on the lookout for a phone call from some other computer. And this is where the trouble begins.

Let's imagine it's very late at night, and everyone in your family has gone to bed. Only the computer is "awake," waiting, as always, for a phone call.

A special signal comes in over the phone line, indicating a call from another computer. The family phones are silent. With their tiny microcomputer brains, they realize the call is not for them.

The computer picks up. It asks the computer at the other end for a password. The other computer is silent for a thousandth of a second, then it blasts a mind-boggling stream of possible passwords at your computer.

Your computer checks each password, attempting to match it with the real password. If there is no match, it signals the other computer "Rejected. Try again." The other computer tries again. And again. And again. And finally it gets it.

Then, in a matter of seconds, the other computer penetrates and takes control of your computer. It scans your computer's directory of private family files. The other computer orders your computer to read the entire contents of each of the files and send it a copy. Your computer is compelled to obey. In a flash, all of your family's intimate and personal information is stored inside the other computer.

Does the other computer sign off now? Not yet. First it inserts a "virus" or "scrambler" program into your computer. Within seconds, the program's destructive work is done. It has randomly recoded every file, every record inside your home computer, into total nonsense, utter gibberish. Your family's information is lost, and there is no way to get it back.

Finally, when your home computer signals the other computer that the scrambler program is done, the other computer orders your computer to erase the program. Then it hangs up.

The next morning, when you sign onto your computer, you discover that all of your family's information has vanished. What happened? Your best guess is a computer memory failure, or, possibly, an error, or bug, in the computer's control program. Little do you realize that you and your family have just been victimized by a new kind of sophisticated criminal, the information burglar.

Fortunately, there will be ways for you and your family to protect your computerized records from electronic intruders and to put a lock on your family computer. One way is a more refined password system. It took the information burglar's computer only a few minutes and a few thousand tries to break the password in the preceding example. Some of the new passwords are so long and so complex, it would take a criminal computer thousands of trillions of tries. This long delay might force the information burglar to give up trying to crack your computer "safe."

Another method of locking your computer, even simpler than the first, would be to have your computer programmed to hang up on the other computer after twenty wrong passwords. But what if the other computer kept calling your computer back? Simple. You could program your computer to sound a burglar alarm in your house whenever it had hung up on another computer five times in the space of five minutes. Alerted to the fact that someone was trying to pry into your computer, you could then temporarily disconnect your computer from the telephone.

A final way to lock your computer would be to use a secret code. You might, for example, write a cryptographic program that would transform all of your family's information into meaningless nonsense. And, since you knew the key to the secret code you were using, you could write a cryptoanalyst program that would turn all of the encrypted information back into understandable form.

But be on your guard. The world's biggest, most sophisticated computers have all been cracked by computer criminals and by ingenious computer programmers. Small, poorly guarded home computers will be easy prey for information burglars. To keep the burglars out of your family's information, you'll need to constantly change the locks and work on making your secret codes more and more difficult to decipher.

REMEMBER BIG BROTHER?

The voice came from an oblong metal plaque like a dulled mirror which formed part of the surface of the right-hand wall. . . . The instrument (the *telescreen,* it was called) could be dimmed, but there was no way of shutting it off completely.

. . . .

The telescreen received and transmitted simultaneously. Any sound that Winston made would be picked up by it; moreover, so long as he remained within the field of vision which the metal plaque commanded, he could be seen as well as heard. There was of course no way of knowing whether you were being watched at any given moment . . . You had to live . . . in the assumption that every sound you made was overheard, and, except in darkness, every movement scrutinized.

George Orwell, *1984*

George Orwell created the "negative utopia" of Oceania in 1949, over thirty years ago. Now, on the eve of 1984, technology has caught up with some of Orwell's most horrifying predictions. The new small computers will make it possible, for example, to have a real life version of the telescreen. Several companies, including Bell Telephone, Sony, and Matsushita, have already built prototypes of telescreens that they are planning to market in the United States. Also, there are numerous electronic mail services that could tie in with a telescreen. These include Picturephone, Viewdata, Teletext, and Qube. All are based on two-way cable or computer-phone-TV linkups now in operation in Europe, Japan, and the United States.

Thousands of homes will soon use telescreenlike devices to tie into the growing electronic network of information and communications. This network will offer many benefits for the citizen and consumer but will represent a two-edged sword. On one hand, individuals and families will be able to use the network to access a wide range of services including electronic newspapers, books, and mail, instant voting, and information on consumer products. Persons who are older, infirm, or handicapped will use the network as a vital link with the outside world.

Unfortunately, along with the benefits will come serious risks. Households will be able to get data from public and private organizations linked to the electronic network, but at the same time these organizations will also have access to the household's computer.

To a certain extent, this will represent a convenience. For example, electronic mail and newspapers can be deposited into the family computer, and banks can automatically balance their customers' checking accounts.

But it goes much further than this. Unless the proper precautions are taken, a family's personal and financial records will be electronically available to insurance companies, credit bureaus, charge card companies, local utilities, prospective employers, department stores, the IRS, law enforcement agencies, and so on.

It is unlikely that a single totalitarian "Big Brother" government will emerge to poke and snoop into the private lives of its citizens. It is possible, however, that there will be numerous "Big Brothers," in the form of corporations and government agencies, who will justify their invasion of people's privacy as a "necessary evil" that enables them to increase efficiency, cut costs, and provide better service. But are these benefits worth the loss of privacy and personal freedom? And is the evil really necessary? These questions will require careful thought in the years to come.

SOME COMPUTER PITFALLS

In less than ten years, many experts predict, there will be a small computer in almost every home. Just having a computer around will change many of us. It will change the way we view ourselves and the world. However, since so many of us will not understand how the computer works or realize its weaknesses or great potential, we will probably run into one of many possible computer pitfalls.

Pitfall 1: The Black Box. Many people are likely to believe manufacturers' claims that the best computer is the easiest to operate—the one with the most prerecorded, canned programs.

Pitfall 2: Gee Whiz! Another group of people—a large group—will be very attracted to home computers and maybe even to those that can be programmed. But once they get the computer home, they will use it exclusively for trivial tasks. They might program the computer to act like a calendar, a notebook, and board game, or a filing cabinet full of files. The computer won't do the tasks any better than the paper calendar or the index-card filing cabinet, but it will be impressive and make the owner feel very efficient.

Pitfall 3: The Crutch. Another group of people will use the computer as a crutch. They'll have it remember things that they are perfectly capable of remembering on their own.

Pitfall 4: The Scapegoat. A large group of people will fall into the pitfall of using the computer as an excuse. They will blame the computer for their own failings and shortcomings.

Pitfall 5: Garbage In, Garbage Out. Most serious of all, instead of acting as a "window on the universe," a small computer will blind some people to the real world. The computer will be used by these people as a prophet, a consultant, a minister, a doctor, an attorney, and so on. In far too many cases, its advice will be mistaken for truth, its opinions mistaken for fact.

There is an old saying among computer people: "Garbage in, garbage out"—GIGO. This is the computer's special failing. Unless you feed it correct information and a program that does exactly what you think it does, the computer is likely to subvert all your intentions and produce nonsense—impressive nonsense, but nonsense all the same.

Pitfall 6: Over My Head Or Just a Snap? Another misconception many people will have about computers is that, to make them work, all you will need to do is plug them in. Curiously, just as many people will think that computers will be so difficult to operate, they'd be better off not even trying. The truth will lie somewhere in between.

Most future computers will be easy to operate. You will turn them on, insert a memory cartridge or cassette, and then issue a verbal command or type something simple on the keyboard.

But it won't be long before you tire of using the canned, prepackaged programs already in the computer. Yet by that time you will also probably be hooked on working with the computer or entertaining yourself with its fast, colorful games. This is exactly the situation the manufacturer wants—a consumer who is bored, addicted, and lazy! It means you are ripe for buying a new canned game or another canned program . . . and another . . . and another. . . .

Let's say instead that you're ready to head out on your own. You want to explore, learn how to program, and create your own games. Unfortunately, though, the going gets rough. You have to take chances. You make mistakes and build models that collapse or come out upside down or backward. You want to give up.

The thing here is to stick with it. The results will be worth it.

Pitfall 7: The Laborsaving Device. There is another group of people who see a small computer as a laborsaving device. This is not a bad view. There is no doubt that many of the most tedious, mindless household chores such as "picking up," vacuuming, dishwashing, and dusting will eventually be done by computers in the form of robots. These are important functions and something for you to look forward to.

But if this is true, shouldn't you use computers to do *all* of your work? Maybe. But only if you want to hang up your thinking cap and let the computer do your thinking for you. Meaningful work can challenge you, give you pleasure, and enrich your life. The computer is best used as a tool to help people in their work, not function as a replacement for the worker. No matter what kind of work you do, chances are the computer can magnify your skills, help you learn new ideas and techniques, and make your work more efficient, more imaginative, more creative, and more interesting.

YOU AND DR. EINSTEIN

Many of the small computers of today produce colorful, action-oriented pictures. But these pictures won't even compare with those that small computers of the future will produce. Various techniques will soon become available to 16- and 32-bit small computers with large-scale memory. These image-generation systems will enable you to create realistic and colorful computer movies using just a few computer commands.

Picture this: A sudden thunderstorm engulfs a tiny plane flying over a Midwest cornfield. A gust of wind slams into the plane and sends it spinning toward the earth. The desperate pilot stares at the instrument panel and clutches the control stick. He yanks the stick backward. Too late. The ground rushes up, and—

No crash. The pilot never left the ground. He wasn't even inside a plane. He was sitting in General Electric's Compu-Scene flight simulator, one of the most advanced image-generation systems in use today. Flight simulators are used to train new pilots without their having to actually fly. GE's system simulates, or imitates, a pilot's aerial view of the earth as seen from the pilot's cockpit window. It looks very much like an animated movie, with one key difference: When the pilot makes a change in the altitude or angle of the plane, the picture changes just as it would if the plane were actually in the air. The computer simulates all sorts of weather conditions, pilot errors, and equipment failures. Pilots get to face a number of frightening air crises without having to risk a real crash landing.

Another exciting system that will one day be available on small computers is Superpaint, an experimental digital video system developed by Dr. Richard Shoup and a team of scientists at Xerox Corporation. Superpaint allows you to create and change animated color images. The images can be incredibly realistic and detailed since they are built from over 300,000 pixels (picture elements) per screen. Superpaint is already being used by NASA to simulate spacecraft maneuvers and experiments underway in outer space.

Superpaint features two picture screens, a light pen, and a data tablet, or digitizer. One screen is your canvas and is empty at the start. On the other screen are your painting materials—brushes (in different shapes and sizes), a palette of many colors of paint, little symbols representing graphic characters, and templates to help you draw straight lines, angles, curves, and other geometric shapes. To paint a picture you merely press the light pen on the color and type of brush you want to use. Then you whisk the pen across your electronic canvas (the picture screen), and the painting appears just as if you had used real paints on real canvas. If you wish to mix your painting with pictures of yourself, say, or a cartoon character, a horse, or an alien creature, you first copy the picture on the screen by tracing it on the data tablet by photographing it with a video camera. Then you can paint over and around the image.

Everything that you draw or copy on the screen can be changed in a variety of ways. Specific objects or areas of the picture can be enlarged, reduced, moved, copied, overlaid, combined, changed in color, erased, or copied to disk or bubble memory for future use. When your painting is complete, you can get a full-color copy of it by pushing a button and sending it from the screen to a laser-driven printer.

Using "graphic languages" of the future, you will be able to create fantastic alien creatures (above) or diagrams of rockets hurtling through space. The Superpaint picture of *Orbiter* (below), created by Xerox for NASA, shows the path the spaceship will follow in a future flight.

Path of Orbiter
Path of
Radar Scan

Many small computers of the future will probably combine the Dynabook computer Xerox is developing with the Superpaint computer. To illustrate how a computer of this kind might be useful, let's say it's about five years in the future, and you are taking a physics course. Your class is studying Newton's principles of mechanics and Einstein's general and special relativity theories, and you are (understandably) having some problems grasping all the concepts.

But you are determined to learn these concepts, or ideas, so you go to the library after classes, pull your Dynabook-Superpaint computer out of the book bag, and start building models that convert the concepts into animated pictures—pictures showing a planet's rotation and its revolution around the sun; pictures of light bending as it passes through the sun's gravitational field; pictures showing the fearsome mass and the awful suction of a black hole or the emission of energy by pulsars and neutron stars; pictures of a spaceship approaching the velocity of light; pictures of solar fusion and atomic fission; and pictures of light as photon particles or oscillating waves.

Like Einstein, you will be performing thought-experiments. But your models won't be rigid or fixed. And as you master new concepts, you can change the models—make them more detailed, realistic, and elaborate—then see the results flash on the computer screen as animated color pictures.

Computers in the future will have high-resolution color graphics, huge memories, lightninglike speed, mathematical and logical skills, and the ability to talk and make sound effects. These are all features that will help you learn difficult ideas and facts you hear in school. You can learn cumbersome Elizabethan poetry by watching and listening to 3-D images of kings and queens in their courts. You can learn organic chemistry by seeing molecules dance. Computers of the future will be windows onto the universe. But you will do more than just see the universe. You will also learn how it works—by using small computers to build universes of your own.

APPENDIX A: SMALL-COMPUTER MAGAZINES

The best way to keep up with all of the new computers, products, games, and programs is to read computer magazines. The major magazines appear monthly and have a large amount of current material in each issue, including complete programs you can copy and run on a small computer. Here are some of the major small-computer magazines, grouped by subject area and by the technical level of their material.*

Games, Learning, and Entertainment

Creative Computing Attractive, full of cartoons, pictures, games and projects, and fun to read. For a single issue or subscription, call (toll-free) 800/631-8112 or write *Creative Computing* magazine, 51 Dumont Place, P.O. Box 789–M, Morristown, NJ 07960.

Recreational Computing Games and projects. For a single issue or subscription, call 415/ 323-3111 or write *Recreational Computing,* People's Computer Company, Box E, Menlo Park, CA 94025.

Beginner's Magazine

OnComputing A good magazine to help you get started. Articles on hardware, software, computer basics, and new products. For a single issue or subscription, call (toll-free) 800/258-5485 or write *OnComputing,* Byte Publications, Inc., 70 Main Street, Peterborough, N.H., 03458.

Home and Business Applications

Interface Age Attractive, easy to read, and full of school, home, and business projects and applications. For a single issue or subscription, call 213/926-9540 or write *Interface Age* magazine, 13913 Artesia Blvd., Cerritos, CA 90701.

---

* All of the magazines listed carry articles on all areas of small computers. This grouping only shows which areas they *emphasize.*

Personal Computing Attractive, fun, easy-to-read articles on school, home, and business computer projects and products. For a single issue or subscription, call 617/232-5470 or write Circulation, *Personal Computing,* Benwill Publishing Corp., 1050 Commonwealth Avenue, Boston, MA 02215.

Programs and Software

Dr. Dobb's Journal A wide-ranging "cookbook" of useful programs—listings, documentation, explanations—for the sophisticated small-computer user. For a single issue or subscription, call 415/323-3111 or write *Dr. Dobb's Journal of Computer Calisthentics & Orthodontia,* People's Computer Company, Box E, Menlo Park, CA 94025.

Advanced Hobbyist or Professional

BYTE An invaluable source of state-of-the-art information for the advanced small-computer user. For a single issue or subscription, call (toll-free) 800/258-5485 or write *BYTE,* Subscriptions, Byte Publications, Inc., 70 Main Street, Peterborough, NH 03458.

Microcomputing A grabbag of practical projects and tutorials for the intermediate-level small-computer user. For a single issue or subscription, call 603/924-7296 or write *Microcomputing,* Subscription Department, P.O. Box 997, Farmingdale, NY 11737.

News about the Latest Products and Technology

InfoWorld If you want to know about small-computer news as soon as it breaks, then you need a small-computer newspaper such as *InfoWorld,* which comes out biweekly (twice a month) and carries the latest developments and news about who's doing what in small computers. For a sample copy or a subscription, write to *InfoWorld,* Circulation Department, 375 Cochituate Road, Route 30, Framingham, MA 01701.

Magazines, Bulletins, and Newsletters

In addition to the major magazines, there are dozens of other magazines, bulletins, and newsletters put out by local computer clubs and by the users and manufacturers of specific models of small computers. For example, there is *80 Microcomputing* (Subscription Services Department, *80 Microcomputing,* P.O. Box 981, Farmingdale, NY 11737), that is devoted to products and programs for owners of Radio Shack's TRS–80 small computer; and *IRIDIS* and *CURSOR,* monthly "cassette" magazines of programs for the Atari 400 and the Commodore PET (same address for both: Box 550, Goleta, CA 93017). To learn more about all of these publications, stop by your local computer store (listed in the Yellow Pages under "Computers" or "Data Processing") or call or write the manufacturer of your favorite small computer.

You can also find dozens of special-interest magazines on specific subjects. For example, if you have a special interest in computer music, you can get a subscription to the *Journal of Computer Music* (People's Computer Company, P.O. Box E, Menlo Park, CA 94025). If you like computer video, movies, graphics, and games, try *Inovision* (from the Inovision Club, P.O. Box 40040, Dallas, TX 75240). If you are interested in robots, there is an excellent magazine called *Robotics Age* (P.O. Box 4029, Houston, TX 77210).

Also, there are numerous "handbooks" on personal computers published by the editors of such magazines as *Popular Mechanics, Mechanix Illustrated, Elementary Electronics, Consumer's Guide,* and so on. These handbooks appear once or twice a year, are reasonably current, and give you a quick introduction to small computers. They are inexpensive and are sold at almost any big newsstand. If you are just getting started, they might be a good purchase.

If you want to keep up with what's happening in small computers but don't want to subscribe to all the magazines, you can send away for the latest *Periodical Guide for Computerists* by E. Berg (E. Berg Publications) through *Bits* (35 Route 101 West, P.O. Box 428, Peterborough, NH 03458). *The Periodical Guide* groups by subject all articles on microcomputers that appeared in over 27 different publications in the preceding years. It is especially helpful if you want to track down recent articles on a particular subject, such as computer art, secret codes, or robots.

Or, you might consider contacting each of the magazines to get their *Cumulative Index and Reprint Catalog,* a subject listing of all the articles ever published by the magazine. You can probably get a copy of the catalog for free.

APPENDIX B: BOOKS ON SMALL COMPUTERS

Dozens of new books on small computers appear every year. Here are some of the better ones, grouped by subject:*

Introduction to Small Computers

Buckwalter, Len. *The Home Computer Book.* New York: Pocket Books, 1978.

Bunnell, David. *Personal Computing: A Beginner's Guide.* New York: Hawthorne Books, Inc., 1978.

D'Ignazio, Fred. *The Creative Kid's Guide to Home Computers.* New York: Doubleday and Company, 1981.

Ledin, George, Jr., and Victer Ledin. *The Programmer's Book of Rules.* Belmont, CA: Lifetime Learning, 1979.

Moody, Robert. *The First Book of Microcomputers: The Home Computer Owner's Best Friend.* Rochelle Park, NJ: Hayden Book Company, Inc., 1978.

Osborne, Adam. *An Introduction to Microcomputers: The Beginner's Book.* Berkeley, CA: Adam Osborne and Associates, Inc., 1979.

Osborne, Adam, *An Introduction to Microcomputers, Volume 1: Basic Concepts.* Berkeley, CA: Adam Osborne and Associates, Inc., 1980.

Sagan, Hans, and Carl Meyer, Jr. *Ten Easy Pieces: Creative Programming for Fun and Profit.* Rochelle Park, NJ: Hayden Book Company, 1980.

Solomon, Leslie, and Stanley Veit. *Getting Involved with Your Own Computer: A Guide for Beginners.* Short Hills, NJ: Ridley Enslow, Publishers, 1977.

Spencer, Donald D. *Microcomputers at a Glance.* New York: Avon, 1977.

Walter, Russ. *Secret Guide to Computers.* 92 St. Botolph Street, Boston, MA 02116: Russ Walter, 1980.

Weisbecker, Joe. *Computer Coin Games.* Morristown, NJ: Creative Computing Press, 1979.

---

* Check the small-computer magazines (see Appendix A) for references to more recent books, especially books on computer music, graphics, computer animation and movies, modeling, and epic fantasy games.

History

Goldstine, Herman H. *The Computer from Pascal to Von Neumann.* Princeton: Princeton University Press, 1972.

Harmon, Margaret. *Stretching Man's Mind: A History of Data Processing.* New York: Mason/Charter, 1975.

Lukoff, Herman. *From Dits to Bits: A Personal History of the Electronic Computer.* Portland, OR: Robotics Press, 1979.

Randall, Brian, ed. *The Origins of Digital Computers: Selected Papers.* New York: Springer-Verlag, 1975.

Rosenberg, Jerry M. *The Computer Prophets.* New York: Macmillan, 1969.

Computers and the Future

Barron, Iann, and Ray C. Curnow. *The Future with Microelectronics: Forecasting the Effects of Information Technology.* New York: Nichols Publishing Company, 1979.

Dertouzos, Michael L., and Joel Moses, eds. *The Computer Age: A Twenty-Year View.* Cambridge, MA: MIT Press, 1979.

Evans, Christopher. *The Micro Millennium.* New York: The Viking Press, 1980.

Graham, Neill. *The Mind Tool: Computers and Their Impact on Society.* St. Paul, MN: West Publishing Company, 1980.

Hiltz, Starr R., and Murray Turoff. *The Network Nation: Human Communication Via Computer.* Reading, MA: Addison-Wesley Publishing Company, 1978.

Martin, James. *The Wired Society.* Englewood Cliffs, NJ: Prentice-Hall, Inc., 1978.

Mowshowitz, Abbe. *The Conquest of Will: Information Processing in Human Affairs.* Reading, MA: Addison-Wesley Publishing Company, 1976.

Nelson, Ted. *The Home Computer Revolution.* South Bend, IN: The Distributors, 1978.

Weiner, Norbert. *The Human Use of Human Beings: Cybernetics and Society.* New York: Avon Books, 1967.

Weizenbaum, Joseph. *Computer Power and Human Reason: From Judgment to Calculation.* San Francisco: Freeman, Cooper and Company, 1976.

Computer Languages

Albrecht, Robert L., LeRoy Finkel, and Jerald R. Brown. *BASIC for Home Computers: A Self-Teaching Guide.* New York: John Wiley & Sons, Inc., 1978.

Bowles, Kenneth L. *Microcomputer: Problem Solving Using PASCAL.* New York: Springer-Verlag, 1977.

Conway, Richard W., David Gries, and E. C. Zimmerman. *A Primer on PASCAL.* Englewood Cliffs, NJ: Winthrop Publishing Co., 1976.

Dwyer, Thomas A., and Margot A. Critchfield. *BASIC and the Personal Computer.* Reading, MA: Addison-Wesley Publishing Company, 1978.
Findlay, William, and David A. Watt. *PASCAL: An Introduction to Methodical Programming.* Washington, DC: Computer Science Press, 1978.
Kernighan, Brian W., and Dennis M. Ritchie. *The C Programming Language.* Englewood Cliffs, NJ: Prentice-Hall, Inc. 1978.
Peelle, Howard A. *APL: An Introduction.* Rochelle Park, NJ: Hayden Book Company, Inc., 1978.
Schoman, Kenneth E., Jr. *The BASIC Workbook: Creative Techniques for Beginning Programmers.* Rochelle Park, NJ: Hayden Book Company, Inc., 1977.
Simon, David E. *BASIC from the Ground Up.* Rochelle Park, NJ: Hayden Book Company, Inc., 1978.
Wegner, Peter. *Programming with ADA: An Introduction by Means of Graduated Examples.* Englewood Cliffs, NJ: Prentice-Hall, Inc., 1980.
Welsh, Jim, and John Elder. *Introduction to PASCAL.* Englewood Cliffs, NJ: Prentice-Hall, Inc., 1979.
Zahn, C. T. *C Notes: A Guide to the C Programming Language.* New York: Yourdon Press, 1979.

Games

Ahl, David H., ed. *BASIC Computer Games: Microcomputer Edition.* Morristown, NJ: Creative Computing Press, 1978.
Ahl, David H., ed. *More BASIC Computer Games.* Morristown, NJ: Creative Computing Press, 1979.
Emmerichs, Jack. *Superwumpus.* Peterborough, NH: Byte Publications, Inc., 1978.
Garrett, Roger. *Starship Simulation.* Portland, OR: Dilithium Press, 1978.
McIntyre, Thomas C. *The A to Z Book of Computer Games.* Blue Ridge Summit, PA: TAB Books, 1979.
Nahigian, J. Victor, and William S. Hodges. *Computer Games for Businesses, Homes and Schools.* Englewood Cliffs, NJ: Winthrop Publishing Co., 1979.
People's Computer Company. *What to Do After You Hit Return, or PCC's First Book of Computer Games.* Menlo Park, CA: People's Computer Company, 1977.
Sage, Edwin R. *Fun & Games with the Computer.* Portsmouth, NH: Entelek, 1975.
Spencer, Donald D. *Fun with Computers and BASIC.* New York: Camelot (Avon), 1977.
Spencer, Donald D. *Game Playing with BASIC.* Rochelle Park, NJ: Hayden Book Company, Inc., 1977.

Models and Simulation

Abt, Clark. *Serious Games.* New York: The Viking Press, 1970.
Boocock, Sarane S., and E. O. Schild. *Simulation Games in Learning.* Beverly Hills, CA: Sage, 1978.

Duke, Richard, ed. *Learning with Simulations and Games:* Beverly Hills, CA: Sage, 1978.
Engel Enterprises and C. W. Engel. *Stimulating Simulations.* Rochelle Park, NJ: Hayden Book Company, Inc., 1979.
Greybeal, Wayne, and Udo W. Pooch. *Simulation: Principles and Methods,* Englewood Cliffs, NJ: Winthrop Publishing Co., 1980.
Lewis, Theodore, and Brian J. Smith. *Computer Principles of Modeling and Simulation.* Boston, MA: Houghton Mifflin Company, 1979.
Maryanski, Fred J. *Digital Computer Simulation.* Rochelle Park, NJ: Hayden Book Company, Inc., 1980.
O'Donovan, Thomas. *GPSS: Simulation Made Simple.* New York: John Wiley & Sons, Inc., 1979.
Osborne, M. R., and R. O. Watts. *Simulation and Modelling.* Lawrence, MA: University of Queensland Press, 1977.

Robots and Artificial Intelligence

George, F. H., and J. D. Humphries, eds. *The Robots Are Coming.* London, England: NCC Publications, 1974.
Heiserman, David L. *Build Your Own Working Robot.* Blue Ridge Summit, PA: TAB Books, 1976.
Hofstadter, Douglas R. *Godel, Escher, Bach: An Eternal Golden Braid.* (Winner of the 1980 Pulitzer Prize for nonfiction). New York: Basic Books, Inc., 1979.
Loofbourrow, Tod. *How to Build a Computer-Controlled Robot.* Rochelle Park, NJ: Hayden Book Company, Inc., 1978.
McCorduck, Pamela. *Machines Who Think: A Personal Inquiry into the History and Prospects of Artificial Intelligence.* San Francisco: W. H. Freeman and Company, 1979.
Raphael, Bertram. *The Thinking Computer: Mind Inside Matter.* San Francisco: Freeman Cooper and Company, 1976.
Reichardt, Jasia. *Robots: Fact, Fiction, and Prediction.* Harmondsworth, Middlesex, England: Penguin Books Ltd., 1978.
Safford, Edward L., Jr. *The Complete Handbook of Robotics.* Blue Ridge Summit, PA: TAB Books, 1978.
Winkless, Nels, and Iben Browning. *Robots on Your Doorstep (A Book about Thinking Machines).* Portland, OR: Robotics Press, 1978.
Winston, Patrick Henry. *Artificial Intelligence.* Reading, MA: Addison-Wesley Publishing Company, 1977.
Young, John F. *Robotics.* New York: John Wiley & Sons, Inc., 1973.

Music

Anderton, Craig. *Electronic Projects for Musicians.* Cupertino, CA: Guitar Player, 1975.
Backus, John. *The Acoustical Foundations of Music.* Second edition. New York: W. W. Norton, 1977.

Hiller, Lejaren A., and Leonard M. Isaacson. *Experimental Music: Composition with an Electronic Computer.* Westport, CT: Greenwood, 1979.
Lincoln, Harry B. *The Computer and Music.* Ithaca, NY: Cornell University Press, 1970.
Mathews, Max, et al. *The Technology of Computer Music.* Cambridge, MA: MIT Press, 1969.
Morgan, Christopher, ed. *The BYTE Book of Computer Music.* Peterborough, NH: Byte Publications, Inc., 1979.

Graphics and Art

Chasen, Sylvan H. *Geometric Principles and Procedures for Computer Graphic Applications.* Englewood Cliffs, NJ: Prentice-Hall, Inc., forthcoming.
Franke, Herbert W. *Computer Graphics—Computer Art,* trans. Gustave Metzger. London, New York: Phaidon, 1971.
Halas, John, ed. *Computer Animation.* New York: Focal Press (Distributed by Hastings House Publications), 1974.
Inman, Don. *Introduction to TRS-80 Graphics.* Portland, OR: Dilithium Press, 1980.
Leavitt, Ruth, ed. *Artist and Computer.* New York: Harmony Books (Distributed by Crown), 1976.
Newman, William N., and Robert F. Sproull. *Principles of Interactive Computer Graphics.* New York: McGraw-Hill, 1979.
Peckham, Herbert. *Computer Graphics.* Palo Alto, CA: The Scientific Press, 1974.
Wadsworth, Nat. *Introduction to Low-Resolution Graphics.* Elmwood, CT: Scelbi Publishers, 1979.

Education and Learning

Ahl, David H., ed. *Computers in Mathematics: A Sourcebook of Ideas.* Morristown, NJ: Creative Computing Press, 1980.
Cauchon, Paul. *Chemistry with a Computer.* Portsmouth, NH: Entelek, 1976.
Fossum, Timothy V., and Ronald W. Gatterdam. *Calculus and the Computer: An Approach to Problem Solving.* Glenville, IL: Scott, Foresman and Company, 1979.
Papert, Seymour. *Mindstorms: Computers, Children, and Powerful Ideas.* New York: Basic Books, Inc., 1980.
Rogowski, Stephen. *Problems for Computer Solution.* Morristown, NJ: Creative Computing Press, 1975.
Spencer, Donald. *Sixty Challenging Problems with BASIC Solutions* (2nd Edition). Rochelle Park, NJ: Hayden Book Company, Inc., 1979.
Walker, Henry M. *Problems for Computer Solutions Using BASIC.* Englewood Cliffs, NJ: Winthrop Publishing Co., 1980.

Computer Crime

Bequai, August. *Computer Crime.* Lexington, MA: Lexington Books, 1978.
Cunningham, John E. *Security Electronics.* Second edition. Indianapolis, IN: Howard W. Sams and Company, 1977.
Leibolz, Stephen W., and Louis D. Wilson. *User's Guide to Computer Crime: Its Commission, Detection and Prevention.* Radnor, PA: Chilton Book Company, 1974.
Parker, Donn B. *Crime by Computer.* New York: Charles Scribner's Sons, 1978.
Whiteside, Thomas. *Computer Capers: Tales of Electronic Thievery, Embezzlement, and Fraud.* New York: Mentor, 1978.

Novels, Poetry, and Short Stories

Ashley, Mike. *Souls in Metal: An Anthology of Robot Futures.* New York: Harcourt Brace Jovanovich (Jove/HBJ Book), 1978.
Asimov, Isaac. *Eight Stories from the Rest of the Robots.* New York: Harcourt Brace Jovanovich (Jove/HBJ Book), 1978.
Asimov, Isaac. *I, Robot.* New York: Fawcett Crest Books, 1950.
Asimov, Isaac. *The Robot Novels.* New York: Doubleday and Company, Inc., 1953, 1954, 1956, 1957.
Bester, Alfred, *The Computer Connection.* New York: Berkeley Publishing Corporation, 1975.
Charbonneau, Louis. *The Intruder.* New York: Doubleday & Company, Inc., 1979.
Gerrold, David. *When Harlie Was One.* New York: Ballantine Books, 1975.
Katz, Leslie George, ed. *Fairy Tales for Computers.* Boston: David R. Godine, Inc., 1978.
McNeil, John. *The Consultant: A Novel of Computer Crime.* New York: Coward, McCann & Geoghegan, 1978.
Paulsen, Gary. *Compkill.* New York: Dell Publishing Company, 1979.
Pohl, Frederik. *Gateway.* New York: Ballantine, 1978.
Pohl, Frederik. *Man Plus.* New York: Bantam, 1977.
Ryan, Thomas J. *The Adolescence of P-1.* New York: Macmillan, 1977.
Van Tassel, Dennie, ed. *Computers, Computers, Computers: In Fiction and in Verse.* New York: Elsevier-Nelson Books, 1977.

GLOSSARY

Acoustic Coupler A device that allows your computer to telephone other computers. See *Modem*.

Add-Ons Accessories or "extras" for a small computer.

Address The storage location of an item in the computer's memory.

Algorithm A list of steps to solve a problem, perform a task, or reach a goal. Algorithms are written in English and then translated from English into computer commands.

Alphanumeric Printer A device that prints letters, numbers, punctuation marks, and special symbols such as $, %, and &; does not print graphic characters, the specially shaped symbols used to draw pictures.

Analog Signal A continuous electrical signal that is an exact reproduction of something (such as temperature, the position of game-control paddles, or sound waves) appearing outside the small computer. Unlike a digital signal (which must be high or low, or on or off), an analog signal can be any frequency, size, or strength.

Analog-to-Digital (A–D) Converter A device that takes an electrical charge and transforms it into a digital charge—a high charge to signify a "1" or a low or zero charge to signify a "0." Small computers process and store commands and information as a series of digital charges (bits). The bits are grouped together, eight at a time, into bytes.

APL (*A* Programming *L*anguage) Developed by Kenneth Iverson in the early 1960s. APL is usually used as an interpreter. APL commands are brief, powerful, and look like mathematical expressions. APL is a good language to use for solving math, science, or logic problems.

Appliance Computer A nonprogrammable special-purpose computer hidden inside an appliance such as an oven, a typewriter, or a digital clock. The computer improves the appliance by making it "solid-state" (with fewer moving parts), more versatile, and "intelligent."

Array Computer There are many types of array computers. One type is built from several microprocessors (computer brains, or CPUs, that fit on a chip). The microprocessors are wired together into an "array" of so many rows and columns. The array computer is extremely fast for two reasons: (1) it can process several commands at the same time; and (2) it can begin processing new information at the same time it is processing old information.

Artificial Intelligence The ability of a machine (such as a robot or a computer) to imitate certain human actions or skills such as problem solving, decision making, perception, and learning.

ASCII (*A*merican *S*tandard *C*ode for *I*nformation *I*nterchange) Most small computers use ASCII to code all information not used in arithmetic. Letters, numbers not used in arithmetic, punctuation marks, other characters such as # and *, and special control signals are all coded in ASCII.

Assembly Language Developed in the early 1950s so that programmers could use abbreviated word commands (pnemonics) in place of the long, confusing strings of ones and zeros that form a computer's machine language. In general, each assembly-language command (such as JMP or ADD) translates into a single machine-language command. The program that does the translating is called an *assembler.*

Audio Device Any computer device that accepts sound or produces sound. Examples include voice-recognition and music or speech synthesis devices.

BASIC (*B*eginner's *A*ll-*P*urpose *S*ymbolic *I*nstruction *C*ode) A high-level language developed by John Kemeny and others at Dartmouth College in the mid-1960s. BASIC is the most popular small-computer language. It is usually implemented as an interpreter, so you can type in commands one at a time and the computer will obey them instantly.

Binary Most small computers are digital computers. This means that all their information and commands are in the form of binary digits (bits) —ones and zeros—that represent high and low (or on and off) charges of electricity. Numbers and all other information not used in arithmetic are coded in ASCII. Numbers used in arithmetic are coded as binary numbers—a way of representing *any* number using only two digits—a "1" and a "0."

Bionic Any combination of machine and living, organic being or part, joined to accomplish a particular task.

Bit (*B*inary Dig*it*) The smallest unit of information inside a small computer. Each bit represents an electrical charge—a "1" represents a high or "on" charge, a "0" represents a low or "off" charge.

Bug An error, or mistake, in a computer program.

Byte A group of eight bits (ones and zeros) representing eight charges of electricity. There are different kinds of bytes: ASCII bytes to represent letters, numbers not used in arithmetic, punctuation marks, etc.; binary bytes that represent numbers used in arithmetic; and command bytes that represent different machine language commands to the computer.

Canned Program Any program written by a manufacturer and stored on a Read Only Memory (ROM). When you use a program on a ROM pack, ROM cartridge, or tape cassette, you are using a canned program. Canned programs are everywhere—inside computerized toys, inside computerized appliances, inside your pocket calculator, and inside your digital watch.

Capacitor An electrical device, or circuit, that stores an electrical charge. Capacitors are often used inside RAM (Random Access Memory). A stored charge in a capacitor represents a "1" bit of information. An absence of a charge in a capacitor represents a "0" bit of information.

Cartridge A circuit board (or card) inside a plastic case with a "plug." On the board are one or more ROM (Read Only Memory) chips. On the chips are programs and information. To get to these canned programs or information, you just plug the cartridge into a slot on the small computer.

Cathode Ray Tube (CRT) A vacuum tube in which a slender beam of electrons is fired onto a fluorescent screen to "draw" a picture, line by line. CRTs are the most common form of video display for today's small computers. However, they will soon be replaced by other devices, such as plasma-ray and LCD screens.

Charge-Coupled Device (CCD) A microelectronic memory similar to RAM or ROM in that it can be placed on a chip. A CCD memory is slower than RAM or ROM, but it can be placed on a smaller chip. CCD memory will probably be used extensively to store images for computer picture screens.

Chip A maze of thousands of miniature wires and circuits, all sitting on a thin slice of silicon about the size of your fingernail. There are many different types of chips in a small computer, each with a particular job to do. The main types of chips are the CPU (Central Processing Unit—or brain) chip; the RAM (Random Access Memory) chip for storing your programs and information; and the ROM (Read Only Memory) chip for storing things such as the computer's control program, an interpreter such as BASIC, games, etc.

Circuit Board A thin, rectangular plastic board on which are mounted one or more chips. There are many types of circuit boards (also called *PC Boards* and *cards*), including memory boards, processor boards, I/O (input/output) boards, etc. However, there are also many single-board computers in which all major parts of the computer (including its CPU, RAM, and ROM chips) are mounted on one board.

COBOL (COmmon Business-Oriented Language) Developed in the late 1950s and early 1960s. A high-level language with commands that resemble English. Especially suited for storing alphabetic and numeric information files and records.

Commands Orders that you give to the computer in the form of words and numbers typed on a keyboard, words spoken into a microphone, positions of a game paddle or joystick, etc.—anything that the computer can understand and obey.

Compiler The program that takes your commands (written in a high-level language such as PASCAL) and translates them into machine-language instructions that can be processed by the computer. A compiler translates all the commands (in a program) together as a single unit.

Computer A machine that accepts, remembers, and carries out a plan or reshapes information. A tool for building models. There are many types of computers, including (1) The general-purpose programmable computer, which can be ordered to follow any rules, perform any task, manipulate any group of symbols, or solve any problem. (2) The special-purpose nonprogrammable computer, which has a single program stored in Read Only Memory. This type of computer is used in computerized toys, weapons, and appliances. Another way of grouping computers is into word-oriented computers (computers that can handle only alphabetic commands and information), number-oriented computers (computers that can handle only numerical commands and data), and alphanumeric computers (computers that can handle both alphabetic and numeric information and commands).

Conductive A quality of a material that allows an electrical charge to pass through it.

CPU (*C*entral *P*rocessing *U*nit) The computer's brain. The CPU obeys one machine-language instruction at a time sent to it by its RAM or ROM memory. All of the sophisticated things a small computer does are based on simple logical and arithmetic operations performed inside the CPU.

Crash When a computer program or computer device stops working abruptly and unexpectedly. A crash often results in a loss of data. It can be caused by a device malfunction or a bug in a program.

Current The flow of electricity—the movement of electrons—through a wire.

Data Information stored or processed by the computer.

Data Security Protection of computerized information by various means, including cryptography, locks, identification cards and badges, restricted access to the computer, passwords, physical and electronic backup copies of the data, and so on.

Data Tablet See *Digitizer.*

Digital-to-Analog (D–A) Converter A device that transforms a computer's digital (high-low or on-off) electrical pulses to continuous analog pulses in order to relay information to or power some device outside of the computer.

Digitizer An A–D Converter that transforms analog electrical signals from a TV camera, light pen, or other device into digital signals that can be stored and processed by a small computer.

Diode Here, a microelectronic device that allows current to flow in only one direction.

Disk A flat, circular object that resembles a phonograph record. A record "stores" music; a disk stores information. A disk is inserted into a disk drive that rotates at high speed. The drive writes new information onto the disk and reads information already stored on the disk. There are two major types of disks found on small computers, flexible floppy disks and hard disks.

Dual In-line Package (DIP) A microelectronic chip rests inside a DIP. The DIP protects the chip and has wires that connect with the tiny wires, or pins, that come out of the chip. The DIP, in turn, plugs into a printed circuit board.

Dynabook A notebook-sized computer that will run on batteries, accept voice input, produce music and voice output, draw realistic, animated pictures, store millions of bits of information, and perform tens of millions of instructions a second.

Electron Gun The heated cathode inside a Cathode Ray Tube that disperses a stream of electrons toward a picture screen.

Error Traps Commands in a program that anticipate people making mistakes when they "talk" to the computer. The commands test people's responses to questions to see if the responses are correct. If not, the commands print an "error message," and the program loops back and asks for another answer.

External Memory Also known as *mass memory* and *removable memory.* External memory is used to store programs and information that would otherwise be lost once the computer was turned off. Examples of external (non-RAM and non-ROM) memory include tape cassettes, disks, bubble, and CCD (charge-coupled) devices.

File A file is a collection of records all appearing under a single file name. All of the programs and data stored in external memory (on tape, disk, bubble, or CCD) are organized into files.

Floppy Disk See *Disk.*

Floppy Disk Drive See *Disk.*

FORTH An interpreter language developed by FORTH, Inc. FORTH programs, in general, are smaller and run faster than the same programs written in BASIC. FORTH programs are especially suited to controlling devices that can be hooked into the computer, such as household appliances, "snooper" sensors, and robots.

FORTRAN Developed in the late 1950s, FORTRAN was the first high-level compiler language. It is widely used, especially in scientific and highly numerical large-computer applications. Shortened versions of FORTRAN run on microcomputers, including the Apple II.

Graphics Pictures as opposed to text.

Grid A method of dividing a computer screen into evenly spaced horizontal and vertical lines. Used for locating points on the screen. These points are expressed as row and column coordinates. The more finely spaced the lines in the grid, the higher the resolution and the more realistic the picture. Each row and column coordinate on the grid represents a single pixel, or picture element, in which a graphics symbol can be placed.

Hardware The machine parts of the computer—the wires, buttons, metal, blinking lights, etc. All of the computer devices.

Heuristic Methods Methods that serve to guide or reveal answers but that cannot be proved.

Holography A technique that, with the use of laser photography, captures a three-dimensional image (hologram) of the photographed subject. Viewers who see the hologram from different angles can also see the subject's image from different angles. Experimental holographic movies are being made in the USSR and in the United States.

Input Device Any machine that allows you to enter commands or information into the computer's main (RAM) memory. An input device could be a typewriter keyboard, an organ keyboard, a tape drive, a disk drive, a microphone, a light pen, a digitizer, or electronic sensors.

Integrated Circuit Any electrical device is really made up of many different "circuit elements" (such as transistors, capacitors, and diodes) that guide and alter the flow of electricity inside the device. Until the 1960s, most of these circuits were built as separate units inside the device, and they took up a lot of space. However, from the 1950s and 1960s on, circuits have been miniaturized and then "integrated," or packed together, onto a single, semiconductor surface such as a silicon chip.

Interface Board A circuit board that allows you to hook the computer up to another machine such as a modem (to make phone calls), a typewriter, the house lights, and so on. The interface board translates the signals from the two devices so that they can communicate with each other.

Interpreter Like a compiler, an interpreter takes your (Englishlike) commands and translates them into machine-language instructions for the computer to process. Unlike a compiler, an interpreter (such as BASIC) will process each command the moment it's entered.

Josephson Junction Two superconductors separated by an insulator. The junction takes the place of a transistor in a Josephson computer and switches electricity down one path or another in as little as six picoseconds—six trillionths of a second. The junctions function only after they have been cooled to almost absolute zero (–459.69° F. or –273.16° C.), a hypothetical temperature characterized by the complete absence of heat.

Josephson Junction Computer An ultrafast computer running on supercooled tunnel junctions in place of transistors. The Josephson computer, when it is assembled, will probably be fifty times faster than today's fastest computers. Since it will require little power to operate, it will generate very little heat. This will allow scientists to pack the whole computer—its brains and memory—into a cube perhaps only 2 inches (5 cm) wide. Yet the computer will be capable of storing millions of bits of information and carrying out a billion operations a second.

Keyboard Set of keys that, when depressed, generate an electrical signal that is transmitted to the computer. There are many kinds of special keyboards, including music keyboards that resemble the keys on a piano or organ and graphics keyboards for drawing pictures on the computer screen.

Language In relation to computers, any unified, related set of commands that can be translated into machine-language instructions the computer can process. There are lower-level languages that are difficult to use but closely resemble the fundamental operations of a computer. There are also higher-level languages that resemble English. In addition, there are specialized languages useful in performing particular tasks, system languages for controlling the operations of the computer, and applications languages that *you* use to write programs. A language is considered to be *extensible* if you can use it to develop new, more powerful language commands on your own.

Lattice A regular crisscrossing arraylike arrangement of atoms in a crystalline substance such as silicon.

LCD (*L*iquid *C*rystal *D*isplay) Small LCDs are used to indicate the time on the faces of digital watches. On computers of the future, large LCDs will be used in place of Cathode Ray Tubes to create flat, high-resolution picture screens.

LED (*L*ight *E*mitting *D*iode) LEDs are commonly used as control lights to indicate whether computer devices are off or on, active or inactive.

Light Pen A device that, when pointed at a computer picture, will generate a command to the computer based on the exact spot where the pen is pointed. The screen might be displaying a menu of commands, the answers to a quiz, or a variety of graphic symbols. You can select the appropriate command, answer, or symbol merely by pointing the pen.

LISP (*LIS*t *P*rocessing Language) As its name indicates, LISP is especially suited to managing and retrieving long, multilevel lists of items. This ability makes LISP a popular language for people who work in the area of artificial intelligence and robotics.

Logic Gate See *Transistor.*

LOGO A computer language, developed by scientists at MIT's Artificial Intelligence Laboratory, that has been used experimentally over the last several years in a children's learning laboratory as a tool to help youngsters master concepts in mathematics, art, and science. The language is simple to learn and contains commands to a cybernetic "Turtle" hooked up to the LOGO computer. LOGO has proven particularly effective as a tool for teaching and communicating with handicapped children, particularly those who are autistic.

Loop A computer is in a loop when it obeys the same instructions in a program over and over. You can use a loop to print your name a thousand times, animate a figure on the picture screen, or repeat a game sequence.

Machine Language A direct representation of electrical charges inside the computer. Machine language was the first computer language. It consists entirely of ones and zeros.

Magnetic Bubbles A magnetic-bubble device, such as CCD, RAM, or ROM, can be placed on a chip. The bubbles are microscopically small, magnetized "domains" that can be moved across a thin magnetic film by a magnetic field. Magnetic-bubble chips have been fabricated that store a million bits of information. Magnetic-bubble memory is not as fast as ROM or RAM but far faster than mass-memory devices such as tapes and disks. Yet like tapes and disks, the information stored inside the magnetized bubbles is retained even after the computer's power is switched off.

Mainframe The box that houses the computer's main memory and logic components—its CPU, RAM, ROM, interface, input-output (I/O) circuitry, and so on.

Mask A plastic keyboard that can be placed on top of the computer's original typewriterlike keyboard. The "keyboard" mask has special keys for composing music, drawing pictures, or playing games.

Mass Memory See *External Memory.*

Microcomputer Originally, a computer that sat on a thumbnail-sized chip of silicon. Now, any small computer whose components (RAM, ROM, and CPU) are on chips.

Millisecond A thousandth of a second.

Model A computer reproduction (or simulation) of a person, process, place, or thing in the real world or in an imaginary world that you create. Models can be simple or complex; artistic, educational, or just for fun; serious or part of a game. To model something, you first learn about it and then you describe it to the computer in the form of a program.

Modem (*Mo*dulator-*Dem*odulator) A device that transforms a computer's electrical pulses into audible tones that are transmitted over a phone line to another computer. A modem also receives incoming tones and transforms them into electrical signals that can be processed and stored by the computer.

MPU (*M*icroprocessing *U*nit) The CPU on a microcomputer.

Multiplexing Transmitting several messages simultaneously over the same circuit or channel; a form of parallel processing.

Multiprocessing A small computer that has more than one CPU and is therefore able to obey several instructions simultaneously; another form of parallel processing.

Multiprogramming A small computer that is able to run more than one program at a time. This allows more than one person to use the computer at a time, and it enables the computer to be engaged in more than one task at a time.

Nanosecond A billionth of a second. Most small computers today have a cycle time, or "heartbeat," of hundreds of nanoseconds. Most high-speed computers have a cycle time of around fifty nanoseconds.

Natural Language A spoken, human language such as English, Spanish, Arabic, or Chinese. In the future, small computers will probably be fast enough and have big enough vocabularies to enable you to talk to them using your natural language. Yet there will still be a need for special computer languages that are more efficient than natural languages in handling certain kinds of tasks.

Network A group of small computers communicating over telephone lines or by use of radio or microwaves.

Operating System A system or control program that gives you a wide range of commands you can use to manage the computer and various input, output, and storage devices. You can use operating-system commands to copy, print, rename, and erase files; to create new files and edit old ones; and to manage file space on external-memory devices such as tape and disk drives.

Optical Wand An input device with a photoelectric "camera" that senses black and white light patterns. Optical wands can be plugged in to computers. Clerks at the check-out counter in your local supermarket may already use an optical wand to read the price of food items. You will be able to use an optical wand to copy program commands into a computer or draw pictures on the computer's screen.

Output Device A machine that takes programs or information from the computer and transfers them to some other medium. Examples of output devices include tape, disk, and bubble-memory drives; computer printers, typewriters, and plotters; the computer picture screen (video monitor); robots; and sound-synthesis devices that enable the computer to talk and play music.

PASCAL A high-level computer language (normally a compiler) named after the seventeenth century French mathematician and philosopher, Blaise Pascal. PASCAL is a more structured and systematic language than BASIC and is suitable for developing complicated model and game programs.

Picosecond A trillionth of a second. Even light, the fastest substance in the universe, can only travel one hundredth of an inch in a trillionth of a second.

Piggyback Signal A secondary signal in the form of electricity, radio waves, and so on, carrying information that is transmitted along with or during a pause in a primary signal.

PILOT An interpreter language, like BASIC and FORTH. PILOT is a simple programming language that is ideally suited for people who are not especially math- or science-oriented.

Pipeline Computer A computer with a string of "processor" CPUs, all capable of executing an operation simultaneously. See *Array Computer* and *Multiprocessing.*

Pixel (from picture element) The computer picture screen is divided into rows and columns of tiny dots, squares, or cells. Each of these is a pixel.

Plasma-Ray Device A flat computer picture screen based on a grid of metallic conductors separated by a thin layer of gas. When a signal is generated at any intersection along the grid, the gas discharges and causes the transparent screen to glow at that point. In the future, the thinner, more reliable, plasma-ray and "solid state" devices will replace CRTs as computer video display terminals.

Platter A hard disk used for computer mass memory.

Plotter A computer device that uses a mechanical arm to draw pictures on paper. The plotter might use colored pens, jets of ink, heating coils, or even a laser beam.

Printed Circuit Board (PCB) A circuit board, or card, is a thin rectangle made of plastic. The top of a PCB contains sockets for DIPs (Dual In-Line Packages) housing the chips, and for components such as diodes and resistors. Printed circuits, or traces, are etched into the PCB to connect all the DIPs and all the separate components. At the end of the PCB are electrical plugs, or contacts, that connect the PCB with the rest of the computer. A "single-board" computer (such as the Atari 400 or Apple II) has only one major PCB. Other "multi-board" computers might be made up of twelve or more PCBs.

Program A combination of one or more computer commands written in a particular computer language. A computer stores and processes a program as a unit.

RAM (*R*andom *A*ccess *M*emory) When you turn on the computer, the thousands of tiny storage cells in RAM are empty (filled with zeros).

Using program and operating-system commands, you can load programs and information into RAM, then relay them from RAM to the CPU where they can be processed. When you turn off the computer, all of the programs and information in RAM are erased.

Record One or more pieces of related information stored in a computer file. Each file can contain one or more records. In a program file, each command in the program is a record. Records can be read from external memory (tape, disk, or bubble), one record at a time, and stored in RAM. After processing, they can be written as part of a file back onto external memory.

Resistance The opposition provided by a wire or circuit element to the passage of a steady electric current.

Resistor A circuit element used to provide resistance for protection, operation, or control of an electric current.

Resolution The number of pixels on the picture screen. A high-resolution picture looks smooth and realistic. It is produced by a large number of pixels (greater than 60,000). A low-resolution picture is blocky and jagged. It is produced by a small number of pixels.

Robot Any stored-program device capable of altering its external environment.

ROM (*R*ead *O*nly *M*emory) ROM chips are found in the computer's mainframe and inside game packs and cartridges that can be plugged in to the computer. Any program or information stored in ROM is instantly available to the CPU for processing. Control programs (including operating systems) are usually stored in ROM; your programming language (such as BASIC or PASCAL) is probably stored in ROM; canned games and other programs are stored in ROM. But ROM is "read only." You can get programs and data from ROM, but you can't erase or change anything stored there.

ROSETTA An early scaled-down version of the SMALLTALK language implemented on 8-bit small computers by scientists of Rosetta, Inc., of Houston, Texas.

Semiconductor A substance midway between an electrical "conductor" and an electrical "insulator." For example, a silicon crystal will not normally conduct electricity. However, when a small amount of another element such as boron or phosphorous is added, silicon becomes a semiconductor and will conduct electricity when a small electrical charge is applied across the crystal. All types of "circuit elements" can be made from a silicon semiconductor, including resistors, insulators, capacitors, diodes, and transistors.

Sensor Any device that acts as "eyes" or "ears" for a small computer. Types of sensors include photoelectric sensors that are sensitive to light; image sensor cameras that record visual images and transform the images into digital signals; pressure sensors that are sensitive to any kind of pressure; contact sensors that are sensitive to touch; infrared sensors that record infrared radiation; and ultrasonic transducers that produce a high-frequency sound wave that bounces off objects and lets the computer calculate the distance between itself and those objects.

Silicon After oxygen, the most abundant element on earth. Most computer chips are made from silicon.

Simulation A computerized reproduction, image, or replica of something else. See *Model.*

SMALLTALK A computer language being developed by the Learning Research Group at the Xerox Palo Alto Research Center. When it finally becomes commercially available, SMALLTALK may well be the most powerful language for small computers of the future.

Software Computer programs.

Subroutine A subroutine is a set of commands invoked by a single, "umbrella" command. The umbrella command appears in the main body of the program, while the detailed subroutine commands appear at the end of the main program.

Superconductive Any material whose resistance to electrical current has been reduced to almost zero.

Synthesizer Any device that produces something based on digital signals stored in the computer. A voice synthesizer produces sounds that closely resemble a person talking. A music synthesizer makes music.

Tape Magnetic voice-grade (audio) tape found on tape cassettes. Used by many small computers as external storage for programs and data. Electrical signals from the computer are transformed into two tones (for a "1" and a "0"), then stored as magnetized segments on the tape. The segments can later be reread, converted into tones, then transformed back into electrical signals that can be stored and processed by the computer.

Telepresence By using all of a robot's sensors, a person can become electronically aware of the robot's immediate environment and control the robot's actions just as if he or she (the person) were actually in that location with the robot.

Telescreen An imaginary device created by George Orwell in his book, *1984.* A telescreen was a two-way, audiovisual "TV" used by a country's rulers to monitor and control the actions of its citizens. Real telescreens are now technologically feasible and are being designed and built by several corporations around the world.

Teletext Textual information transmitted to people's homes via their TV. Information is usually maintained and updated on a computer. A teletext system often allows two-way interaction by creating a viewer-computer link over a telephone line.

Teletypewriter (TTY) A computer typewriter. Used by many deaf people (without a computer connection) to make phone calls. TTYs are quickly being replaced by devices such as the C-Phone (a small computer), which are faster and much more versatile.

Time-Sharing Occurs when a single computer has multiple users who are each getting a "slice" of each second of the computer's processing time.

Transistor A microelectronic circuit element made from a semiconductor such as silicon. Transistors inside a small computer form switches that turn electricity on and off, amplifiers that increase an electrical charge, and, ultimately, logic gates that enable the computer to perform arithmetic, make decisions, and juggle symbols such as letters and words.

Tunnel Junction See *Josephson Computer* and *Josephson Junction.*

Turing Test A test devised by the computer scientist, Alan Turing, to determine if a machine is "intelligent." Essentially, if a human observer cannot tell whether he or she is in the presence of a machine or a person, the machine is judged to be "intelligent."

Videodisk A silvery, recordlike device storing a large amount of audio and visual information that can be linked to a computer. A single side of one videodisk can store the pictures and sound for 54,000 separate TV screens. Yet any one of these screen images can be accessed and displayed on a real screen in, at most, 2.5 seconds. In the future, games and models can combine computer animation and sound effects along with the pictures and sound from a videodisk.

Video Terminal A computer picture screen and keyboard.

VLSI (*V*ery *L*arge-*S*cale *I*ntegration) The number of logic gates (decision-making and processing circuits) that can be packed onto a chip. Already, 11,000,000 logic gates can be squeezed on a chip surface the size of the human brain. With the next step of circuit miniaturization—ULSI (Ultra Large-Scale Integration)—this number will jump dramatically.

INDEX

ABOUT THE AUTHOR

Fred D'Ignazio is a free-lance writer, programmer/analyst, and Ph.D. candidate in computer science at the University of North Carolina at Chapel Hill. He has written two previous books on the subject of computers, *Katie and the Computer* (Creative Computing Press, 1979), a science fantasy picture book, and *The Creative Kid's Guide to Home Computers* (Doubleday & Co., 1981), a collection of computer games and projects for older children.

Fred is married and has two children.